Income Distribution, Market Imperfections and Capital Accumulation in a Developing Economy

"I find this book very interesting. Prior to Asim Dasgupta's work, the standard growth and development models ignored credit constraints and their implications for resource allocations and growth. This had disturbing implications: a redistribution of income from the rich to the poor would lower savings and investment, thus capital accumulation and growth. But redistributions in a credit constrained world may lead to a more efficient allocation of capital, thereby improving growth.

While the findings are intuitive, *Income Distribution, Market Imperfections and Capital Accumulation in a Developing Economy* presents a simple and convincing model to establish them with some rigor. The exposition is sufficiently clear that it should be easy to follow."

—Joseph E. Stiglitz, *American economist and Professor at Columbia University, USA. He is also a recipient of the Nobel Memorial Prize in Economic Sciences (2001) and the John Bates Clark Medal (1979).*

Asim K. Dasgupta

Income Distribution, Market Imperfections and Capital Accumulation in a Developing Economy

palgrave
macmillan

Asim K. Dasgupta
Former Finance Minister
West Bengal, India

Former Professor of Economics
Calcutta University
West Bengal, India

ISBN 978-981-13-1632-6   ISBN 978-981-13-1633-3 (eBook)
https://doi.org/10.1007/978-981-13-1633-3

Library of Congress Control Number: 2018953330

© The Editor(s) (if applicable) and The Author(s) 2018
This work is subject to copyright. All rights are solely and exclusively licensed by the Publisher, whether the whole or part of the material is concerned, specifically the rights of translation, reprinting, reuse of illustrations, recitation, broadcasting, reproduction on microfilms or in any other physical way, and transmission or information storage and retrieval, electronic adaptation, computer software, or by similar or dissimilar methodology now known or hereafter developed.
The use of general descriptive names, registered names, trademarks, service marks, etc. in this publication does not imply, even in the absence of a specific statement, that such names are exempt from the relevant protective laws and regulations and therefore free for general use.
The publisher, the authors and the editors are safe to assume that the advice and information in this book are believed to be true and accurate at the date of publication. Neither the publisher nor the authors or the editors give a warranty, express or implied, with respect to the material contained herein or for any errors or omissions that may have been made. The publisher remains neutral with regard to jurisdictional claims in published maps and institutional affiliations.

Cover illustration: Pattern © Melisa Hasan

This Palgrave Pivot imprint is published by the registered company Springer Nature Singapore Pte Ltd.
The registered company address is: 152 Beach Road, #21-01/04 Gateway East, Singapore 189721, Singapore

*To the Memory of
My Parents*

Foreword

In this important investigation on economic progress, Asim Dasgupta has drawn attention to a number of overlooked aspects of development planning that demand greater exploration. Dasgupta is particularly focused on the inadequacy of capital accumulation in traditional economies, including peasant societies. He notes that the belief that inequality reduction must be a regressive step for development because it would pull down capital accumulation (allegedly because of the lower propensity to save of the poor) arises from the error of missing the connection between inequality reduction and institutional changes favourable to—indeed necessary for—stimulating economic development. Nor must we overlook the dependence of market imperfections, so inimical to development, on social inequalities. Through exploring these—and other—neglected connections, Dasgupta has very substantially broadened our understanding of the process of development that must pay much more attention to institutional change.

Recipient of Nobel Prize in Economics
and now Thomas W. Lamont University
Professor at Harvard University

Amartya Sen

Preface

This book is a part of my PhD thesis at the Massachusetts Institute of Technology, USA (1975). Soon after my return to India, I got involved in the functioning of the newly elected Left Front Government in West Bengal (1977–1978 to 2010–2011), first, in the preparation of Annual Economic Reviews of the State, then as the Minister of Finance, Development and Planning, and also for some time, Minister for Excise and Urban Development, and finally as the Chairman of the Empowered Committee of Finance Ministers of all the States in India (2000–2001 to 2010–2011). Along with these responsibilities, I have also tried to carry on teaching (in honorary capacity) as Professor in the Department of Economics of Calcutta University, which included, among others, introduction of a new course on Development Management involving fieldwork and guidance to the students for dissertation every year.

While involvement in all these spheres delayed the work on publication of my book, this involvement at the same time helped me enormously in getting insight into the working of a real-life economy and also confirming the ground-level acceptability of the main idea of the thesis, related as it is, to the interaction between the distribution of income and the process of development itself.

For this entire process of learning, I remain grateful to my teachers at Kolkata—at Presidency College as well as at Calcutta University—Professor Sukhomoy Chakravarty, Professor Bhabatosh Datta, Professor Amiya Bagchi, and Professor Prabuddha Nath Roy, and also to my colleague Professor Arup Mallik.

At the Massachusetts Institute of Technology, I benefited significantly from my discussions with Professor Robert Solow, Professor Jagdish Bhagwati, and Professor Richard Eckaus, and my contemporary researcher Dr M.L. Agarwal. Later on, discussions especially with Professor Amartya Sen have provided new insights.

Interactions with the students, particularly at Calcutta University, and with the representatives of working people—peasants and workers at the ground level—have also been a new kind of learning experience.

West Bengal, India   Asim K. Dasgupta

Acknowledgements

Ms Sagarika Ghosh, Senior Editor, and Ms Sandeep Kaur, Assistant Editor, at the Palgrave Macmillan Publishing Group have been particularly helpful, keeping at the same time a healthy pressure regarding deadlines. I wish to thank them especially.

Mr Phalguni Mookhopadhayay, my former student and now the Chancellor of Brainware University, Barasat; Mr Monoj Mukherjee and Mr Sanjib Biswas of the same University helped me with technical assistance. I wish to record my appreciation for this assistance. For similar help, I remain thankful to Mr Anindya Bhattacharya.

My brother, Professor Atis Dasgupta, former professor and head of Sociological Research Unit at the Indian Statistical Institute, Kolkata, has encouraged me throughout my research and other activities. My two daughters, Isha and Ujani, had to suffer due to my involvements outside. I could not attend to their needs adequately as they were growing up. But they never allowed the bond of affection to slacken.

My deepest gratitude is to my wife, Syamali, who stood by me during my research work and all other involvements, bearing the entire burden of holding everything together. No amount of formal thanksgiving would be a full expression of my gratitude to her. I know she understands it.

About the Book

There are different ways in which attempts have been made to try to explain the problem of insufficient capital accumulation and growth in a less developed country. In the conventional analyses, this explanation is often attempted in terms of socio-cultural factors, such as attitudes towards saving and investment, irrationality of peasant behaviour, technological issues of externalities, and demographic factors. In this book, an alternative explanation has been presented in terms of the distribution of assets and incomes. It has been shown that given an unequal distribution of assets and incomes and the resulting market imperfections, especially credit market imperfection, in many developing countries, the income groups that can and in fact do save may not use their savings for capital accumulation, not necessarily because of any socio-cultural reasons, technological and demographic obstacles, but simply because that will go against the maximisation of their very rational objective related to net income or utility. One advantage of this kind of approach is that it can go a longer way in explaining the problem of capital accumulation in terms of economic variables. It can also draw our attention to a different kind of constraints—constraints of political-economic in nature—on economic developments, which are very different from the ones suggested in the conventional analyses.

Three short statements about the benefits of reading this book:

1. This book brings out the importance of distribution of assets and incomes as factors in explaining the problem of insufficient capital accumulation and growth in an underdeveloped economy, and

through that it brings into open the political-economic factors lying behind the issue of continued underdevelopment.
2. The book focuses on the significance of political-economic factors, not in isolation but along with the conventional issues, such as those related to the technical progress and vicious cycle of poverty. This accommodation of two types of explanatory factors has been couched in terms of a comprehensive model worked out in this book.
3. As a result of this inclusion of both types of explanatory factors—institutional and technological—the book makes it possible to work out a more complete package of policies in terms of which government and other appropriate agencies can fruitfully intervene.

Contents

1 Introduction   1

2 Characteristics of the Economy   3

3 The Model   11

4 Behaviour of the System over Time   37

5 Significance of the Distribution of Income and Structure of Credit Market   51

6 Different Ways of Resolving the Crisis   59

7 Some Other Results in the Literature   69

8 Generalisations   73

Index   77

About the Author

Asim K. Dasgupta stood *first* in *First Class* in MA in Economics from Calcutta University (1966). Joined as a lecturer in Economics Department, Calcutta University, in 1967.

Dasgupta took study leave and completed PhD Programme in Economics with Widrow Wilson Fellowship at the Massachusetts Institute of Technology, USA (1970–1975). While working on PhD programme, he also taught at College of Business Administration, Boston University (1973–1974), and was adjudged to be the best teacher in terms of students' evaluation.

After returning to India (1975), Dr. Dasgupta joined teaching at the Department of Economics, Calcutta University, and got promoted to the post of Reader and then Professor. While performing duties as Minister of Finance, Excise and Development & Planning (1987–1988 to 2010–2011), he kept on teaching on honorary capacity once a week and introduced a new course named Development Management, which included a compulsory study tour and dissertation by the students.

As a Minister of Finance, Excise and Development & Planning, he played an important role in introducing Decentralised Planning with the participation of people through the elected local bodies—Panchayats and Municipalities in West Bengal.

He has been the first Chairman of the Empowered Committee of Finance Ministers of the States, elected and reelected unanimously by all the States' Finance Ministers over the period 2000–2010, and played a significant role, in cooperation with other State Finance Ministers and the Union Finance Minister, in introducing Value Added Tax (VAT) in the States (2005–2006), and then also in formulating the basic structure of Goods and Services Tax (GST) for both the Centre and the States (2009–2010).

CHAPTER 1

Introduction

Abstract In this book, an explanation of insufficient capital accumulation in a developing economy is offered in terms of the distribution of assets and income. It is shown that given an unequal distribution of assets and income and the resulting market imperfections, especially credit market imperfection, in many developing countries, the income groups which can and in fact do save may not use their savings for capital accumulation.

Keywords Conventional analyses • Alternative explanation
• Distribution of assets and income • Market imperfection

The main theme will be developed within the agricultural sector of a developing economy, and then it will be pointed out how this can be extended to cover the industrial sector as well. In Chapter 2, the major characteristics of such agriculture are described, stressing particularly the dualism that exists between the family and capitalist farms, the distribution of income between them, and the implication of that distribution for the structure of rural credit market. Given these characteristics, a model is developed in Chapter 3, by deriving the decision rules that the family and capitalist farms will adopt about the use of inputs and allocation of wealth on the basis of some well-defined maximising objectives. In Chapter 4, this model is then used to analyse the special problem of capital accumulation

© The Author(s) 2018
A. K. Dasgupta, *Income Distribution, Market Imperfections and Capital Accumulation in a Developing Economy*,
https://doi.org/10.1007/978-981-13-1633-3_1

in this agriculture. It is found that given an unequal initial distribution of income and the associated imperfection of credit market, such agriculture can show a tendency to approach a state of zero rate of capital accumulation under very plausible conditions, and this can be accompanied by a process of immiserisation of family farms. The importance of the distribution of income and the structure of credit market as factors responsible for this crisis is brought out more precisely in Chapter 5, where the results of this model are compared with those of a hypothetical situation involving a more equal distribution of income and a more perfect credit market. In Chapter 6, several ways of resolving this crisis are discussed, including particularly the solution that is offered by technical progress. Here, it is found that the issues connected with a special kind of technical progress, namely, the Green Revolution, as well as those connected with some other solutions based on institutional changes, can be given an interesting interpretation. In Chapter 7, the conclusions of this model are compared with other existing results in the literature. Finally, several ways of generalising the basic model are suggested (Chapter 8). It needs also to be pointed out at the outset that certain assumptions of our model, made particularly about the nature of market imperfections, are based primarily on the characteristics prevailing in the Indian agriculture. But in this respect, the Indian situation may not be very atypical of peasant agriculture of many other less developed countries.

References

Bhaduri, A. (1983). *The Economic Structure of Backward Agriculture*. Cambridge, MA: Academic Press.

Leibenstein, H. (1957). *Economic Backwardness*. New York: Wiley.

CHAPTER 2

Characteristics of the Economy

Abstract The main theme is developed within the agricultural sector of a developing economy. Later, it is pointed out how this can be extended to cover the industrial sector as well. In this chapter, the major characteristics of such agriculture are described, stressing particularly the dualism that exists between the family and capitalist farms, the distribution of income between them, and the implication of that distribution for the structure of rural credit market.

Keywords Allocational decision rules • Production and Consumption loans

Consider an economy with an agricultural and an industrial sector. Although the primary concern of this presentation is with the agricultural sector, it is worthwhile in the beginning to comment very briefly on the structure of industrial sector as well, particularly its links with the agricultural sector, so that results derived within the agricultural sector can be viewed from the perspective of the entire economy.

The industrial sector is divided into a private sector producing a luxury consumption good, to be consumed partly in the industrial sector and partly in the agricultural sector, and a government sector producing a capital good to be used again in both sectors. The agricultural sector, in its turn, produces a necessary consumption good—a part of it is consumed within agriculture and another part goes to industry. The other link between the two sectors is through the labour market. It may be further noted that the credit market linkage between the two sectors in rather weak. Even now, of the total credit disbursed by the scheduled commercial banks, 91.6 per cent is in urban areas and only 8.4 per cent in rural areas.[1]

Given this structure of the entire economy, we shall, as indicated before, concentrate on the agricultural sector. In order to be able to do that, we choose, for most of this presentation, not to go into the problems of interaction between agriculture and industry. It will be assumed that the agricultural output can be sold at a fixed (money) price within the sector and also to industry, and so also can be the luxury consumption good produced by industry. Capital goods are also available to the agricultural sector at a fixed price from the industrial sector and migration of labour from agriculture to industry is not significant. It will be mentioned later how all these assumptions can be relaxed and results generalised, but to start with they help us to focus our attention on the agricultural sector.

Within the agricultural sector, an important feature observed in many less developed countries is the coexistence of the family and capitalist farms. The distinction between the two is based on the significance of hired labour in the total labour force used in the respective farms. The family farm uses labour mostly of its family members, whereas the capitalist farm is dependent primarily on the wage labour coming from the family farms. For the sake of simplicity, we will assume in our analysis that the family farm uses only the family labour and the capitalist farm only the wage labour from the family farms.[2] The distribution of land between these two types of farms is given at any point of time, and there does not exist any significant market for land. By this it is meant that there does not exist any market for voluntary exchange of land. One important reason for this is that in a society exposed to various kinds of risk, and with a few means of insurance effectively available, land is a highly attractive asset to

---

[1] Reserve Bank of India, Quarterly Report of Scheduled Commercial Banks, September to December, 2016.

[2] In agriculture, in addition to those two classes, there is also a class of landless agricultural labourers. In India, for example, according to the National Sample Survey (2013), landless agriculture labour households constitute 7.4 per cent of the total agricultural households. To begin with, this landless labour will not be considered in our analysis, but it will be shown later how its existence can be accommodated into the basic model without much change in analysis.

hold. In particular, to a farmer on the margin of subsistence, who is most likely to be the potential seller of land, the risk of parting with land is often one of starvation and land prices rarely fully reflect this risk as evaluated by the farmer. However, although there does not exist any voluntary exchange of land, "distress sale" of land does take place. In fact, it will be shown later that it is through such a mechanism that the capitalist farm can take over the ownership of land from the family farms in some special situations, such as default of loan by the latter. But until a family farm is driven to such an extreme situation, the total amount of land owned by a family does not get voluntarily exchanged.

Now, the size of this land holding of a family farm is usually quite small compared to a capitalist farm. Consistent with the census findings, if the small and marginal farms (with a land holding size of five acres and less) are taken to be characterised as the family farm and the large farm as the capitalist farm, then according to the recent study conducted by the National Council of Applied Economic Research (NCAER 2010, Table 6.5), the average income of the family farm is much lower than that of the capitalist farm, both in relative sense (about one fourth) and also in absolute sense (less than Rs 9,000 per annum). This distribution of income between the family and capitalist farms—the significant disparity between their average incomes as well as the low absolute value of the family farm's income—is to be taken as the description of the initial state in our analysis. And, as we shall presently see, this has an important implication for the structure of agricultural credit market. For that, one has to look into, among other things, the nature of the production process in agriculture.

The production process in agriculture can be best described by continuous input-point output technology. The entire process takes place over an interval of time which can be called an agricultural "year" and can be taken to be equal to a "period" in our analysis. Within each such period, starting from the beginning point and spread over the entire interval, labour and capital are applied by both the family and capitalist farms to their given amounts of land, and then output is obtained at the end point of the period. The production function is assumed to be neoclassical showing constant returns to scale and diminishing returns to factors, and is the same for both the farms. However, the decisions they have to take on the use of labour and capital, though related, are not the same.

Consider, first, the family farm. It starts any period with a certain amount of family labour and a net income obtained from the previous period. Of this family labour, a part is to be used in its own production and the rest to be sent away to work on the capitalist farm for wage which, we assume, is paid <u>post facto</u>. By the net income of the previous period is meant the gross income of that period which, because of the nature of agricultural production and of wage payment, was obtained at the end point of the period, less the amount of loan that was taken in that period and had to be paid back. As already documented, the average gross income of the family farm is very low and hence its average net income is even lower. From the available empirical evidence, we find it reasonable to assume that from this level of average income it is not possible for the family farm to save anything. The family farm, therefore, does not own any stock of capital; it has to take production loan for using capital. Not only is the average net income of the family farm low to rule out saving, but very often it is also inadequate to meet the per head consumption needs of the family over the entire production period. Since wage is paid at the end of the period, this implies that the family farm has to take loan also for consumption purposes.[3]

All these loans are taken from the capitalist farm and under conditions of an imperfect credit market. The cause and the nature of this imperfection will be explained shortly. What needs to be carefully mentioned is that after a certain amount of loan has been taken at a given rate of interest by the family farm, it has to allocate this loan between the uses for consumption and production, and this allocation can be done only with respect to a well-defined objective function. This will be precisely shown in Chapter 3.

Using these loans, the family farm produces its output at the end of the period. This output, evaluated at the fixed market price, together with the wage earned from the capitalist farm, determines the gross income of the family farm for this period. The net income is then obtained by deducting from the gross income the loans which have been taken in this period and which, in our analysis, are always supposed to be paid back at the end of the period. It is with this net income, the total and the corresponding average, that the family farm starts the next period. Along with the net income, there is also a different size of labour force supplied in the next period, and the rate of growth of this labour force is considered as exogenously given.

---

[3] The analysis does not change in any essential way if wage is considered to be paid in advance. Then an interest is charged on this wage and therefore, in effect, wage becomes a part of the consumption loan. It can be checked that the conclusions of this chapter are invariant with respect to the nature of wage payment.

We like to point out now that, to begin with, it is helpful to suppose that the average net income of the family farm, though small, is positive.[4] This means that although the family farm could not save and had to take loans because its average net income at the beginning point of the period was small, and the output and wage earnings were not to be available until the end of the period, and during this period the family had to take care of its consumption needs as well as keep the production going with rented capital, yet when the output is finally obtained and wage income received, it can indeed pay back those loans and is left with some positive average net income with which it can start the next period. That is, in the beginning, there is no problem of defaulting to worry about.

The interesting question, then, is: what happens over time? Does this average net income increase or stay constant, and therefore remain positive? Or, does it fall over time, threatening a bankruptcy of the family farm? How does the capitalist farm react to that situation? The purpose of this presentation is precisely to answer these questions, by analysing the intertemporal behaviour of the average net income of the family farm vis-à-vis the capitalist farm and then relating that to the entire question of capital accumulation.

Let us now turn to the capitalist farm. Like the family farm, the capitalist farm also starts any period with a given number of family members and a net income from the previous period. But, there are two important differences. First, the members of the capitalist family do not work and labour is hired for production from the family farm. Secondly, the average net income of the capitalist farm is much higher than that of the family farm, and with this higher level of income the capitalist farm can both consume

---

[4] Nothing is altered in our basic analysis or in the final conclusion if the net income of the family farm is non-positive to start with. It will be demonstrated in Chapter 4 that, under certain plausible conditions, a dualistic agriculture can show an inherent tendency to approach a limiting state with respect to capital accumulation and impoverishment of the family farm. A situation of non-positive net income of the family farm simply means, as will be evident later on, that from the standpoint of analysis, this situation is even simpler to tackle since in this case one can skip certain intermediate steps. We think, however, that it is not enough to analyse only this terminal stage as it may relate to a dualistic agriculture, it is also necessary to understand and explain the historical process by which such an agriculture is actually brought to this terminal stage. That is why we have decided to start with an initial situation which is somewhat away from this terminal stage, being characterised by a positive net income for the family farm. The situation with a non-positive net income of the family farm will then come to be analysed incidentally as a part of the more complete analysis of the evolutionary process.

and save. Its consumption is on the agricultural product as well as on the luxury consumption good from industry, both of which are assumed to be available at fixed prices. More important than consumption is the fact that the capitalist farm can save, something which the family farm could not do, and this saving when added to the pre-existing stock of wealth gives the total wealth of the capitalist farm for the present period. The capitalist farm can keep this wealth in two forms: (a) capital to be used in its own production, and (b) loan to be given to the family farm.[5] This choice of portfolio, of course, has to be made with respect to a well-defined objective function, and this will be shown in Chapter 3.

The capitalist farm, thus, combines two operations at the same time—production and lending—and it is to be noted that in the market for the latter there exists an imperfection. This imperfection in the credit market arises primarily because of the special nature of the distribution of income and wealth already mentioned, whereby there are numerous family farms with a low level of average income and wealth, and therefore in need of credit, and a relatively few capitalist farms with a much higher level of average income and wealth, and in a position to supply that credit. These relatively few capitalist farms, again, are found to be spread over the entire agricultural sector with the result that within a local credit market there exists a typical situation of many family farms facing one (or very few, but homogeneous enough to be considered one) capitalist farm as the money lender.[6]

This monopolistic position of the capitalist farm in the credit market is also reinforced by the lack of any serious competition from the conventional commercial banks. This is because there are some special problems connected with assessing the credit worthiness of the family farms, arising mainly from their low income and wealth position, and the commercial banks, located as they are in the urban areas, are at a serious disadvantage in handling these problems. Very often, therefore, it is found that the participation of the commercial banks in the agricultural credit market is

---

[5] It should be noted that the capitalist farm has control only over the amount of loan to be given to the family farm at a certain rate of interest. Beyond that, it does not have any control on the final allocation of that loan between production and consumption. That allocation is done only by the family farm and in accordance with its own objective function, as has already been mentioned.

[6] It is an interesting exercise to prove how starting with an initial distribution of income such as has been considered here, the relatively few capitalist farms will find it most profitable to have themselves spread over the entire sector so that each one can enjoy a monopolistic hedge in its local credit operation.

practically negligible.⁷ This is a job which the local capitalist farmer, due to his intimate knowledge of the economic positions of the family farmers, is uniquely suited to perform, and, here, he can outcompete not only the urbanised commercial banks but also the other capitalist farmers who are not strictly local.

An appropriate stylised way of characterising the agricultural credit market is therefore to describe it in terms of a representative set which is sufficiently localised and consists of several family farms and one capitalist farm, with the latter enjoying a virtual monopoly in the local lending activity. And the agricultural sector can then be visualised as the union of numerous such sets which are not only significantly insulated from the credit market of the industrialised urban sector but also non-intersecting among themselves so far as credit operations are concerned. It should be noted, however, that this non-intersection is meant to apply only for the credit market. With respect to the labour market, for example, there is no such isolation, the relevant market being the entire agricultural sector itself.⁸

Given this structure, the capitalist farm has, at the end of the period, two sources of income—one is the value of output produced with its own capital and hired labour, and the other is the interest earnings from loan. These two kinds of income can be added up to get the gross income of the capitalist farm, and its net income is then obtained by deducting from this the wages to be paid to the hired family farmers. The capitalist farm begins the next period with this net income, the total and the corresponding average. Meanwhile, the size of its family has grown over the period, the rate of growth, as in the case of the family farm, being determined exogenously.

This is a description of a dualistic agriculture with the family and capitalist farms, their initial distribution of income, the implication of that distribution on the structure of credit market, and the general nature of the decisions they have to take on the use of inputs and allocation of wealth. The purpose of this analysis is to derive these decision rules in a

---

⁷ It is crucially important to mention here the finding of a recent Task Force set up by the Government of India on credit-related issues of farmers. "The limited access of small and marginal farmers to institutional credit continues to be matter of concern and that proportion of such farmers is increasing and they form more than four-fifth of the total operational holdings" (Report of the Task Force on credit Related Issues of Farmer, Ministry of Agriculture, Government of India, 2010).

⁸ Later on, in Chapter 8, we shall discuss briefly the possibility where imperfection of the credit market may also imply a monopsony in the labour market whereby the family farmers may be forced to work only for the local capitalist-cum-money lender.

precise form and analyse them in relation to the particular question of capital accumulation. For that, the objectives of the two farms are to be stated precisely, and, in this context, we assume that both the farms in making their allocation decisions are guided by the objective of maximising the happiness of their respective family members, not only within one period, but also over a certain span of periods, and express this objective as a discounted sum of utility defined over a stipulated time horizon and relating to consumption per head of the family members of the respective farms. This intertemporal characterisation of the objective, it should be noted, is essential if the decision rules with respect to saving and accumulation of wealth are to be accounted for. It should also be noted that although on grounds of analytical completeness we shall work with this Ramsey-type intertemporal objective functional and derive the decision rules subject to that, most of these rules can also be derived, as will be shown later in Chapter 3, from a somewhat simpler specification of the objective, namely, that the family and capitalist farms try to maximise their net income (i.e., profit) in any period with an additional intertemporal requirement that the net income of any period should not fall below that of the previous period.

Decision making with reference to an objective function, specified in either of these two forms, can be regarded as the usual expression of rational behaviour in economic analysis. And, as pointed out at the very outset, our intention in this analysis is to offer an alternative explanation of the agricultural stagnation of a less developed economy on the basis of such a framework of rational behaviour on the part of both the family and capitalist farms, but as applied to the very special objective circumstances of a dualistic agriculture which arise primarily from its state of distribution of income and the related structure of the credit market.

References

National Council of Applied Economics Resources (NCAER). (2010). Table 6.5.
National Sample Survey, Government of India. (2013). *Landless Agricultural Labourers in India*.
Report of the Task Force on Credit Related Issues of Farmers, Ministry of Agriculture, Government of India. (2010).
Reserve Bank of India, Quarterly Report of Scheduled Commercial Banks, September to December, 2016.

CHAPTER 3

The Model

Abstract Keeping the characteristics of dualistic agriculture in view, a model is developed by deriving the decision rules that the family and capitalist farms will adopt about the use of inputs and allocation of wealth on the basis of certain well-defined maximising objectives.

Keywords Net income of family farm • Net income of capitalist farm

As indicated in the previous chapter, the agricultural sector can be considered as divided into numerous sets consisting of the family and capitalist farms, and these sets can be regarded as non-intersecting in their credit operations. Suppose, for the sake of simplicity, that there are m such identical sets (m is sufficiently large, but finite) and within each set there are n identical family farms and one capitalist farm (or, a few of them, homogeneous enough to be regarded as one unit). With this notion of aggregation, we now proceed to derive the allocational decision rules, first for the family farm and then for the capitalist farm, taking into account all the structural characteristics as already mentioned. It is these rules that will define the model of our analysis.

The Family Farm

Given the nature of agricultural production and the relationship between the processes of income generation for the two types of farms, as outlined in the previous chapter, the total income of a family farm belonging to such a representative set in period t can be written as

$$Y_1(t) = \bar{P} F\left(\bar{T}_1, K_1(t), L_1(t)\right) + w(t) L_2(t) \\ - i(t)\bar{P}_k K_1(t) - \left(1 + i(t)\right)\bar{P} C_1^l(t), \tag{3.1}$$

where $Y_1(t)$ is the total net income of the family farm in period t, $\bar{P}$ is the fixed money price of the agricultural output which is produced subject to a neoclassical production function F showing constant returns to scale and diminishing return to factors, $\bar{T}_1$ is the given amount of land which remains unchanged except in the case of default of loan, $K_1(t)$ is the amount of capital rented from the capitalist farm, $\bar{L}_1(t)$ is the labour of family members used in its own production, $L_2(t)$ is the family labour sent away for work in the capitalist farm and $w(t)$ is the money wage rate thereof. The first two terms on the R.H.S. of (3.1) add up to give the total gross income of the family farm. $\bar{P}_k$ the fixed price of capital, $\bar{P}C_1^l(t)$ the money value of the consumption loan and $i(t)$, the rate of interest for period t, so that the last two terms of (3.1) are the rental payment on the production loan and interest-plus-principal payment on the consumption loan respectively.

There are certain issues in connection with the production and consumption loans which are worth clarifying at the outset. In the first place, there is a difference in the way the two loans are paid back in each period. Since the services of capital can be rented per period, the payment of production loan in any period in the absence of depreciation is just the payment of rental. The consumption loan, on the other hand, is like wages fund; it cannot be used without it being exhausted, and hence the payment of consumption loan includes both principal and interest. Second, given the continuous input-point output technology, capital needs to be rented in the beginning of the period and used in production over the entire period. The consumption loan, on the other hand, need not be taken right in the beginning of a period. Depending on the amount of net income available from the previous period, it can be taken at any time within the period, but naturally before the end point when the output is again available. Since we have used the same rate of interest for both kinds of loan, it should be understood that an initial adjustment has been made for the rate of interest on the consumption loan, so that it can refer to the entire period. Finally, it should be noted that we shall very often add up $\bar{P}_k K_1(t)$ and $\bar{P}C_1^l(t)$ to define the total loan of the family farm in any period t, and there is no stock-flow contradiction involved. Note that the total loan of the family farm in any period t is: $\sum_{\tau=-\infty}^{\tau=t}\bar{P}C_1(\tau) + \sum_{\tau=-\infty}^{\tau=t-1}\bar{P}_k \Delta K_1(\tau)$. But, in our analysis, it is assumed that loans are paid back at the end of each year, so that

$$\sum_{\tau=-\infty}^{\tau=t-1}\bar{P}C_1^l(\tau) = 0$$

Therefore with $K_1(t)$ denoting the capital stock covering the entire period t, the total loan of the family farm in any period t can be written as: $\bar{P}_k K_1(t) + \bar{P}C_1^l(t)$.

Given the total net income of the family farm, as defined in (3.1), its average net income in period t is:

$$y_1(t) = \frac{Y_1(t)}{\bar{L}_1(t)} = \frac{\bar{P}F\left(\bar{T}_1, K_1(t), L_1(t)\right) + w(t)L_2(t)}{\bar{L}_1(t)} \qquad (3.2)$$

$$- \frac{i(t)\bar{P}_k K_1(t) + \left(1 + i(t)\right)\bar{P}C_1^l(t)}{\bar{L}_1(t)},$$

where $\bar{L}_1(t)$ is the size of the family and, for the sake of simplicity, is also taken to be its total labour force.[1]

$$L_1(t) + L_2(t) = \bar{L}_1(t) \qquad (3.3)$$

It is assumed that $\bar{L}_1(t)$ grows at an exogenously fixed rate g:

---

[1] Alternatively, one can assume that the labour force is a certain fixed proportion $0 < \alpha < 1$ of $\bar{L}_1(t)$.

$$\bar{L}_1(t) = \bar{L}_1(0)(1+g)^t, \ g > 0 \qquad (3.4)$$

As already explained in detail, the net income with which the family farm starts any period is low so that it cannot save and has to rent capital and also take consumption loan to meet the consumption requirement.[2] Therefore, denoting by $c_1(t)$ the consumption per head of the family in real terms, we can write

$$c_1(t) = \frac{y_1(t-1)}{\bar{P}(1+g)} + \frac{C_1^l(t)}{\bar{L}_1(t)} \qquad (3.5)$$

These are the definitions of the relevant variables as applied to the family farm and the definitional equations involving them. The question, now, is: how does the family farm make its choice about the value of these variables, L_1, K_1, and C_1^l when its objective, as mentioned at the end of the last chapter, is to maximise a discounted sum of utility relating to per capita consumption of its family members over some stipulated time horizon, that is, to maximise

$$\sum_{0}^{T_1} \lambda_1^{-t} U(c_1(t)) \qquad (3.6)$$

where T_1 is the length of time horizon for the family farm, $\lambda_1 (>1)$ is the discount factor for its time preference, U is its instantaneous utility function with required concavity, and $c_1(t)$ is defined by (3.5).

---

[2] We have already mentioned it before (cf. p. 4n), and we repeat it here, that for our analysis and final conclusions it is not essential that saving of the family farm be zero and the amount of its consumption loan positive. What we need is a situation where, because of the existing distribution of income, the family farm cannot save enough and it has to take some loan from the capitalist farm, be it consumption loan or renting of capital (in other words, the credit market should be allowed to remain in the picture). Given such an upperbound on saving on the part of the family farm properly defined, it can be shown just by using the property of imperfection of the credit market and the stated objectives of the farms that, under very plausible conditions, the system will evolve over time in such a way that after a certain period of time the saving of the family farm will in fact drop to a negligible amount and that it will also have to take consumption loan. And, the present analysis applies from then on. Therefore, the assumptions of zero saving and positive consumption loan on the part of the family farm are not analytically essential.

This is essentially a discrete analogue of the generalised Ramsey problem, and the Euler conditions for maximum[3] in this discrete-time case are obtained by constructing the following sum of two adjacent terms of the utility functional,

$$Z_1 = \lambda_1^{-t} U\left[\frac{y_1(t-1)}{\bar{P}(1+g)} + \frac{C_1^I(t)}{\bar{L}_1(t)}\right] + \lambda_1^{-(t+1)} U\left[\frac{F(\bar{T}_1, K_1(t), L_1(t))}{\bar{L}_1(t+1)}\right. \quad (3.7)$$
$$\left. + \frac{w(t)(\bar{L}_1(t) - L_1(t))}{\bar{P}\bar{L}_1(t+1)} - \frac{i(t)\bar{P}_k K_1(t)}{\bar{P}\bar{L}_1(t+1)} - \frac{(1+i(t))C_1^I(t)}{\bar{L}_1(t+1)} + \frac{C_1^I(t+1)}{\bar{L}_1(t+1)}\right],$$

and then setting the partial derivatives of Z_1 with respect to the relevant arguments, $L_1(t)$, $K_1(t)$, and $C_1^I(t)$ equal to zero[4]:

$$\bar{P} F_{L1}(\bar{T}_1, K_1(t), L_1(t)) = w(t) \quad (3.8)$$

$$\frac{\bar{P}}{\bar{P}_k} F_{K1}(\bar{T}_1, K_1(t), L_1(t)) = i(t) \quad (3.9)$$

$$\lambda_1 U'\left[\frac{y_1(t-1)}{\bar{P}(1+g)} + \frac{C_1^I(t)}{\bar{L}_1(t)}\right] - \left[\frac{1+i(t)}{1+g}\right] U'\left[\frac{F(\bar{T}_1, K_1(t), L_1(t))}{\bar{L}_1(t)(1+g)}\right.$$
$$\left. + \frac{w(t)(\bar{L}_1(t) - L_1(t))}{\bar{P}\bar{L}_1(t)(1+g)} - \frac{i(t)\bar{P}_k K_1(t)}{\bar{P}\bar{L}_1(t)(1+g)} - \frac{(1+i(t))C_1^I(t)}{\bar{L}_1(t)(1+g)} + \frac{C_1^I(t)}{\bar{L}_1(t)(1+g)}\right] = 0, \quad (3.10)$$

where

$$F_{L1} = \frac{\partial F()}{\partial_{L1}}, \quad F_{K1} = \frac{\partial F()}{\partial K_1} \quad \text{and} \quad U'() = \frac{dU(c_1())}{dc_1()}$$

Note that (3.8) and (3.9) are the static optimality conditions which give the family farm's decision rules with respect to the use of labour and

---

[3] The second-order Legendre condition is satisfied by the concavity of utility function.
[4] For a discussion of the Euler conditions in the discrete-time case, see P.A. Samuelson, "A Turnpike Refutation of the golden Rule in a Welfare-Maximising Many-Year Plan" in (R.C. Metron ed.) *The Collected Scientific Papers of Paul A. Samuelson*, Vol. 3, pp. 108–110.

capital respectively. In making these decisions, the family takes w and i as parameters. The wage rate is determined by the aggregate supply of labour from all the family farms and the aggregate demand for labour from all the capitalist farms of the agricultural sector taken together, while the rate of interest is set within a representative set monopolistically by the capitalist farm. An individual family farm acting alone cannot affect either w or i.

The condition (3.10), on the other hand, is the dynamic optimality condition (an analogue of the Ramsey rule for the problem of the family farm) which has to hold for any pair of adjacent periods $(t, t+1)$, and it gives us the demand function of the family farm for the consumption loan, $\bar{P}C_1^l$.

It is a second-order difference equitation embedded in the optimal time profile of $\bar{P}C_1^l$, and it is known that such a profile is uniquely fixed by the initial and the terminal conditions relating to $\bar{P}C_1^l$.

We choose to specify these conditions by two constants, to be denoted by B_1 and B_2. Given these specifications, for any period t, the value of $\bar{P}C_1^l$ obtained from the previous period (which, incidentally, is zero because of the assumption that the loan of any period is to be paid back in that period) as well as that related to the next period, $\bar{P}C_1^l(t+1)$, can be taken as predetermined, and it is then possible to characterise the demand function for $\bar{P}C_1^l$ for any period t as:

$$\bar{P}C_1^l(t) = \psi\left(i(t), w(t), y_1(t-1), \bar{L}_1(t); \lambda_1, g, B_1, B_2\right), \quad (3.11)$$

where the variables, $K_1(t)$ and $L_1(t)$, are eliminated by virtue of (3.8) and (3.9), and, g, B_1, and B_2 are the given constants. Now, by using the implicit function rule with respect to (3.10), it can be easily seen, as is also intuitively expected, that

$$\psi_1 = \frac{\partial \bar{P}C_1^l(t)}{\partial i(t)} < 0, \quad \psi_2 = \frac{\partial \bar{P}C_1^l(t)}{\partial w(t)} > 0,$$

$$\psi_3 = \frac{\partial \bar{P}C_1^l(t)}{\partial y_1(t-1)} < 0 \text{ and } \psi_4 = \frac{\partial \bar{P}C_1^l(t)}{\partial \bar{L}_1(t)} > 0.$$

In the same way, it can also be verified that the elasticities of $\overline{PC}_1^l(t)$ with respect to $i(t)$ and $w(t)$, to be denoted by $e_{\psi,\,i}$ and $e_{\psi,\,w}$, are inversely related with the value of the discount factor, λ_1, and those with respect to $y_1(t-1)$ and $\overline{L}_1(t)$ to be denoted by e_{ψ,y_1} and $e_{\psi,\overline{L}_1}$ are directly related with λ_1.

Of particular importance for our later analysis is the comparison between $e_{\psi,\,i}$ and e_{ψ,y_1}. At a low level of income, when the consumption is more of a necessity than luxury, it is reasonable to expect that in any period the elasticity of $\overline{PC}_1^l$ with respect to the net income available in that period is significantly higher than that with respect to the rate of interest to be paid on the loan.[5] A good way of presenting this phenomenon in terms of our analytical framework is through an appropriate valuation of λ_1. Since at a very low level of income, an individual is expected to be especially concerned about its immediate, rather than future, consumption, one can consider λ_1 of the family farm as having a significantly high value. And, given the qualitative nature of the relationship of $e_{\psi,\,i}$ and e_{ψ,y_1} with λ_1 as just mentioned, such a high value of λ_1 can then be taken to imply a correspondingly high value of e_{ψ,y_1} compared to $e_{\psi,\,i}$.

We now make a short digression on a related issue, which is of some concern in the literature on development, bearing on the decision of the family farm with respect to L_1 (and, therefore, also L_2) and a possible imperfection of the labour market. It is often mentioned that there exists a positive gap between the wage rate at which labour can be hired from the family farm and the marginal product of labour in the family farm.[6] It is interesting to see that this situation can be easily accommodated in terms of our framework of analysis. One important reason behind the existence of this wage gap, it is believed, is the fact that when the members of the family farm, particularly the women, work in their own farm they can coordinate and combine farm work with domestic chores, something which they are unable to do when at work as a hired labour on the capital-

---

[5] For similar reason e_{ψ,y_1} will also dominate $e_{\psi,\,w}$ since wage is supposed to be received at the end of the period.

[6] See, Bhagwati, J. and Chakravarty, S. "Contributions to Indian Economic Analysis: A Survey," *American Economy Review*, 59, No. 2 Suppl. (September 1969); Sen, Amartya K.: "Peasants and Dualism with or without Surplus Labour," *Journal of Political Economy*, October 1966.

ist farm.⁷ What this means in terms of our analytical framework is that there is an opportunity cost associated with L_2 being sent away to work at the capitalist farm. If $\mu(t)$ is taken to denote this opportunity cost per unit of $L_2(t)$, then (3.2) can be rewritten as

$$y_1(t) = \frac{\bar{P} F(\bar{T}_1, K_1(t), L_1(t)) + (w(t) - \mu(t)) L_2(t)}{\bar{L}_1(t)} - \frac{i(t) \bar{P}_k K_1(t)}{\bar{L}_1(t)} - \frac{(1 + i(t)) \bar{P} C_1^I(t)}{\bar{L}_1(t)} \quad (3.2')$$

and (3.8) as

$$\bar{P} F_{L1}(\bar{T}_1, K_1(t), L_1(t)) = w(t) - \mu(t) \quad (3.8')$$

There will be a similar modification of (3.10) so that (3.11) can be rewritten by including $\mu(t)$ as another argument:

$$\bar{P} C_1^I(t) = \psi\left(i(t), w(t), y_1(t-1), \bar{L}_1(t), \mu(t); \lambda_1, g, B_1, B_2\right)$$
$$\text{with } \partial \bar{P} C_1^I(t) / \partial \mu(t) < 0. \quad (3.11')$$

It is now clear from (3.8') that so long as $\mu(t) > 0$, $w(t) > \bar{P} F_{L1}$ and therefore the wage gap.⁸ The value of $\mu(t)$ can be considered as depending on $L_2(t)$ and $\bar{L}_1(t)$:

---

⁷ See, Bardhan, P.K., Loc. cit. pp. 1379–1381. For empirical evidence in the Indian context, see Visaria, P., "The Farmers' Preference for Work on Family Farms," in *Report of the Committee of Experts on Unemployment Estimates*, New Delhi, Govt. of India, 1970.

⁸ There is an alternative explanation of the wage gap, due to Lewis (cf. his "Economic Development with Unlimited Supplies of Labour". *Manchester School of Economics and Social Studies*, May 1954), which suggests that the peasant leaving his family to work outside loses his income from the farm, equal to the average product per person, and the wage rate outside must compensate for this. This explanation can also be accommodated in our analytical framework. Note that for this argument to be valid, it is necessary to assume that the outgoing peasant cannot rent out or sell his share in the land held by the joint family, that the family refuses to subsidise him with remittances, and that he does not remit back his wages. What all this means is that when the peasant goes out in this way, he, in effect, ceases to be a member of the family. To capture this situation, therefore, the wage term in the expression of net income of the family should be dropped, and then the wage rate of the outgoing

$$\mu(t) = \mu\left(L_2(t), \bar{L}_1(t)\right)$$

where $\partial\mu(t)/\partial L_2(t) > 0$, since the opportunity cost increases as more of family labour goes out to work in the capitalist farm, and $\partial\mu(t)/\partial\bar{L}_1(t) < 0$, since there are economies of scale associated with a larger size of the family. But $d\bar{L}_1/dt > 0$ and, also generally, $d\bar{L}_2/dt > 0$. Hence the sign of $d\mu/dt$ is ambiguous. We start by assuming that the two effects tend to cancel out each other so that μ can be taken not to change over time, and then see later on how the results will have to be qualified if μ is considered to change in one way or other. For the purpose of our immediate analysis, therefore, (3.11′) will be written as:

$$\bar{P}C_1^I(t) = \psi\left(i(t), w(t), y_1(t-1), \bar{L}_1(t); \mu(t), \lambda_1, g, B_1, B_2\right), \quad (3.11'')$$

with μ treated as a constant.

It should be carefully noted in this context that the existence of a wage gap, as described above, is quite consistent with the imperfections of both the land market and capital market which we have previously specified. With the imperfection of labour market thus accommodated and the Eqs. (3.2), (3.8), and (3.11) accordingly modified by (3.2′), (3.8′), and (3.11″), the optimal decision rules for the family farm are given by (3.8′), (3.9), and (3.11″).

Let us now turn to the capitalist farm to find out its corresponding optimal decision rules.

The Capitalist Farm

Recalling that there are n identical family farms and one capitalist farm within a representative set (of the family and capitalist farms), the total net income of the capitalist farm in any period t can be written as:

peasant indeed becomes equal to the average net income of the family farm. It should be emphasised, however, that this explanation of the wage gap, based as it is on a particular kind of relationship between the outgoing peasant and the family, is more appropriate for the rural-urban migration than for the allocation of family labour between its own farm and the capitalist farm within agriculture. In this context see also Stiglitz, Joseph: "Rural-Urban Migration, Surplus Labour and the Relationship between Urban and Rural Wages," *East African Economic Review*, December 1969, and "Wage Determination and Unemployment in L.D.C.'s," *The Quarterly Journal of Economics*, May 1974.

$$Y_2(t) = \bar{P} F\left(\bar{T}_2, K_2(t), n L_2(t)\right) - w(t) n L_2(t) + i(t) M(t), \qquad (3.12)$$

where Y_2 is the total net income, $\bar{P}$ is the fixed money price at which the agricultural product can be sold by both the capitalist and the family farm, F is the production function available to both of them, $\bar{T}_2$ is the given amount of land which again remains unaltered until the capitalist farm takes over the land of the family farm in the event of a default of loans, $K_2(t)$ is the capital stock owned by the capitalist farm and used in its own production, and $M(t)$ is the total loan given by the capitalist farm to n identical family farms, that is,

$$M(t) = n\bar{P}_k K_1(t) + n\bar{P} C_1^l(t) \qquad (3.13)$$

Note that while the family farm's repayment of the consumption loan, for reasons already mentioned, has to include both the principal and interest and therefore the amount to be deducted from its gross income on this account is $(1+i(t))\bar{P} C_1^l(t)$, the definition of the capitalist farm's flow of income in any period, on the other hand, can include only the interest earnings on the loan, whether the loan is for consumption or production.

The average net income of the capitalist farm can then be written as:

$$y_2(t) = \frac{Y_2(t)}{\bar{L}_2(t)} = \frac{\bar{P} F\left(\bar{T}_2, K_2(t), n L_2(t)\right) - w(t) n L_2(t)}{\bar{L}_2(t)} + \frac{i(t) M(t)}{\bar{L}_2(t)}, \qquad (3.14)$$

where $\bar{L}_2(t)$ is the size of the capitalist family which, like that of the family farm, grows at an exogenously fixed rate g:

$$\bar{L}_2(t) = \bar{L}_2(0)(1+g)^t, \; g > 0 \qquad (3.15)$$

Unlike the family farm, however, the capitalist farm can save and this saving in period t, when added to its wealth already existing from the previous period, $A_2(t-1)$, defines the total wealth of the capitalist farm in period t, $A_2(t)$. Therefore, consumption per head of its family members in real terms for period t can be written as:

$$c_2(t) = \frac{y_2(t-1)}{\bar{P}(1+g)} - \frac{A_2(t)}{P\bar{L}_2(t)} + \frac{A_2(t-1)}{P\bar{L}_2(t)} \qquad (3.16)$$

Now, we know that for any value of $A_2(t)$, however determined, the capitalist farm can hold this wealth in terms of two kinds of assets: capital to be owned and used in its own production and loans to be given to the family farms, so that

$$A_2(t) = \overline{P}_k K_2(t) + M(t) \qquad (3.17)$$

These are the definitions of the relevant variables for the capitalist farm and the definitional equations involving them. Given these, the problem of the capitalist farm is to choose the values of the variable $L_2(t)$, $K_2(t)$ and $M(t)$ (and, given (3.17)), also $A_2(t)$ so as to maximise the discounted sum of utility relating to the per head consumption of its family members over a stipulated time horizon, that is, maximise

$$\sum_0^{T_2} \lambda_2^{-t} U(c_2(t)), \qquad (3.18)$$

where T_2 and λ_2 are the time horizon and the discount factor for the capitalist farm, and $c_2(t)$, its real per head consumption, is defined by (3.16). Note that the instantaneous utility function, U, has been considered to be the same (with required concavity) for both the family and capitalist farms.

The Euler conditions for maximum are then obtained by setting the partial derivatives of the sum of typical adjacent terms of the series,[9]

$$\begin{aligned} z_2 = \lambda_2^{-t} U & \left[\frac{y_2(t-1)}{\overline{P}(1+g)} - \frac{\overline{P}_k K_2(t) + M(t)}{\overline{P}\,\overline{L}_2(t)} + \frac{A_2(t-1)}{\overline{P}\,\overline{L}_2(t)} \right] \\ + \lambda_2^{-(t+1)} U & \left[\frac{F(\overline{T}_2, K_2(t), nl_2(t))}{\overline{L}_2(t)(1+g)} - \frac{w(t) n L_2(t)}{\overline{P}\,\overline{L}_2(t)(1+g)} \right. \\ & \left. + \frac{i(t) M(t)}{\overline{P}\,\overline{L}_2(t)(1+g)} - \frac{A_2(t+1)}{\overline{P}\,\overline{L}_2(t)(1+g)} + \frac{\overline{P}_k K_2(t) + M(t)}{\overline{P}\,\overline{L}_2(t)(1+g)} \right] \end{aligned} \qquad (3.19)$$

with respect to $L_2(t)$, $K_2(t)$, and $M(t)$, respectively, equal to zero:

---

[9] The second-order conditions are again taken care of by the concavity of U.

$$\bar{P} F_{L2}(\bar{T}_2, K_2(t), nL_2(t)) = w(t) \tag{3.20}$$

$$\lambda_2^{-t} U'(c_2(t)) \left[-\frac{\bar{P}_k}{\bar{P}\bar{L}_2(t)} \right] + \lambda_2^{-(t+1)} U'(c_2(t+1))$$
$$\left[\frac{F_{k2}(\bar{T}_2, K_2(t), nL_2(t))}{\bar{L}_2(t)(1+g)} + \frac{\bar{P}_k}{\bar{P}\bar{L}_2(t)(1+g)} \right] = 0 \tag{3.21}$$

$$\lambda_2^{-t} U'(c_2(t)) \left[-\frac{1}{\bar{P}\bar{L}_2(t)} \right]$$
$$+ \lambda_2^{-(t+1)} U'(c_2(t+1)) \left[\frac{i(t)\left(1 - \frac{1}{e(t)}\right) + 1}{\bar{P}\bar{L}_2(t)(1+g)} \right] = 0, \tag{3.22}$$

where $F_{L2} = \frac{\partial F()}{\partial nL_2}$, $F_{k2} = \frac{\partial F()}{\partial K_2}$ and $e = -\frac{\partial M}{\partial i} \frac{i}{M}$ is the elasticity of the aggregate demand for loan with respect to the rate of interest, the aggregate demand being obtained by adding up the demand for consumption and production loan over all the family farms in the representative set.

Clearly, (3.20) is the optimal rule for choosing $L_2(t)$, while (3.21) and (3.22) can be combined to yield:

$$\frac{\bar{P}}{\bar{P}_k} F_{k2}(\bar{T}_2, K_2(t), nL_2(t)) = i(t)\left(1 - \frac{1}{e(t)}\right)$$
$$\text{Or, } \theta(t) \frac{\bar{P}}{\bar{P}_k} F_{k2}(\bar{T}_2, K_2(t), nL_2(t)) = i(t) \tag{3.23}$$

where $\theta(t) = \frac{1}{1 - 1/e(t)}$, and this gives the capitalist farm's rule of allocating any given amount of $A_2(t)$ between $M(t)$ and $\bar{P}_k K_2(t)$.

The optimal rule for choosing the amount of $A_2(t)$ can then be derived in the following way. Given (3.17), $\partial z_2/\partial A_2$ can be expressed as a linear combination of $\partial z_2/\partial k_2$ and $\partial z_2/\partial M$:

$$\frac{\partial z_2}{\partial A_2} = \frac{\partial z_2}{\partial M} + \frac{1}{P_k}\frac{\partial z_2}{\partial k_2} \tag{3.24}$$

Now, substituting the values of $\partial z_2/\partial M$ and $\partial z_2/\partial k_2$ from (3.21) and (3.22), $\partial z_2/\partial A_2$ can be set equal to zero to obtain:

$$\lambda_2 U'\left[\frac{y_2(t-1)}{\bar{P}(1+g)} - \frac{A_2(t)}{\bar{P}\bar{L}_2(t)} + \frac{A_2(t-1)}{\bar{P}\bar{L}_2(t)}\right] - \left[\frac{\frac{i(t)}{\theta(t)}}{1+g} + 1\right]$$

$$U'\left[\frac{F(\bar{T}_2, K_2(t), nL_2(t))}{\bar{L}_2(t)(1+g)} - \frac{w(t)nL_2(t)}{\bar{P}\bar{L}_2(t)(1+g)}\right. \tag{3.25}$$

$$\left. + \frac{i(t)M(t)}{\bar{P}\bar{L}_2(t)(1+g)} - \frac{A_2(t+1)}{\bar{P}\bar{L}_2(t)(1+g)} + \frac{A_2(t)}{\bar{P}\bar{L}_2(t)(1+g)}\right] = 0$$

which is a second-order difference equation embedded in the optimal time profile of A_2.[10] It is known that this profile is uniquely fixed by the initial and the terminal condition relating to A_2, and we shall specify these by two constants, to be denoted by D_1 and D_2. With these specifications, for any period t, the values of $A_2(t-1)$ and $A_2(t+1)$ can be taken as given, subsumed in these specifications, and then (3.25) can be used to characterise the capitalist farm's holding of A_2 in the period as:

$$A_2(t) = f\left(\frac{i(t)}{\theta(t)}, y_2(t-1), \bar{L}_2(t); \lambda_2, g, D_1, D_2\right) \tag{3.26}$$

where the other variables in (3.25) are eliminated by virtue of (3.20) and (3.23), and $\lambda_2, g, D_1,$ and D_2 are the given constants. Note that because of the monopolistic position of the capitalist farm in the credit market, its decision to hold $A_2(t)$ depends, among others, on the marginal rate of return, $i(t)/\theta(t)$, rather than on the average rate of return, $i(t)$. Clearly,

---

[10] Equation (3.25) can be regarded as the analogue of the Ramsey rule for the problem of the capitalist farm.

under a competitive situation, $\theta(t) = 1$ and these two rates of return would be the same.

By using the implicit function rule to (3.25), one can verify what one intuitively expects about the signs of the partial derivatives of f, that is,

$$f_1 = \frac{\partial A_2(t)}{\partial \frac{i(t)}{\theta(t)}} > 0, \quad f_2 = \frac{\partial A_2(t)}{\partial y_2(t-1)} > 0 \text{ and } f_3 = \frac{\partial A_2(t)}{\partial \bar{L}_2(t)} > 0.$$

In the same way it can also be found that the elasticity of $A_2(t)$ with respect to $i(t)/\theta(t)$, $e_{f,i/\theta}$ is inversely related with λ_2 and those with respect to $y_2(t-1)$ and $\bar{L}_2(t) e_{f,y/2}$ and $e_{f,i/\theta} \bar{L}_2$ are directly related to λ_2. Of particular importance for our later analysis is the comparison between the difference of the income and the rate return elasticities of A_2 for the capitalist farm, $(e_{f,y_2} - e_{f,i/\theta})$ and difference of the corresponding elasticities of $\bar{P}C_1^l$ for the family farm, $(e_{\psi,y_1} - e_{\psi,i})$. Since the average level of income of the capitalist farm is significantly higher than that of the family farm, and accordingly the consumption of the capitalist farm is less determined by the consideration of necessity, it is reasonable to expect that the difference between e_{f,y_2} and $e_{f,i/\theta}$ for the capitalist farm will be significantly smaller than the corresponding difference between e_{ψ,y_1} and $e_{\psi,i}$ for the family farm.

A good way of presenting this phenomenon in terms of our analytical framework is again through an appropriate stipulation of λ_2 in relation to λ_1. Since $y_2(t-1)$ is significantly higher than $y_1(t-1)$ and the standard of living of the capitalist farm is way above the state of existence of the family farm, the preference pattern of the capitalist farm will be significantly less biased for the immediate consumption than what it is/was for the family farm. In other words, one can stipulate $\lambda_1 > \lambda_2$, and, given the relationship of e_{ψ,y_1} and $e_{\psi,i}$ with λ_1 and that of e_{f,y_2} and $e_{f,i/\theta}$ with λ_2 and the structural similarity between ψ and f, this difference between λ_1 and λ_2 can be taken to imply a corresponding difference between $(e_{\psi,y_1} - e_{\psi,i})$ and $(e_{f,y_2} - e_{f,i/\theta})$, that is

$$(e_{\psi,y_1} - e_{\psi,i}) > (e_{f,y_2} - e_{f,i/\theta}) \tag{3.27}$$

We find therefore that the capitalist farm's decision to hold its total wealth, $A_2(t)$, is given by (3.26), and its decision to allocate that wealth between $M(t)$ and $\bar{P}_k K_2(t)$, which is taken simultaneously with the deci-

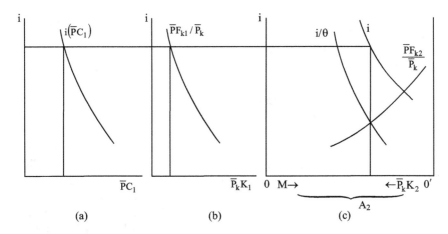

Fig. 3.1 Allocation of wealth

sion to hold $A_2(t)$, is given, as already mentioned, by (3.23). This allocation of $A_2(t)$ between $M(t)$ and $\bar{P}_k K_2(t)$ along with the consequent determination of the rate of interest and, given that rate of interest, the final allocation of this loan, $M(t)$, by each family farm between the uses of consumption and production all are shown in Fig. 3.1(a–c).

In going through these figures, it should be kept in mind that this is a depiction of the working of only the asset-cum-credit market of a dualistic agriculture. This is not a full general equilibrium picture, because, to keep the diagram simple, we have not shown the interactions with the labour market explicitly. From (3.11″) it is clear that, given other arguments, the demand of a typical farm for the consumption loan can be related with the rate of interest as shown in terms of the $i(\bar{P}C_1^l)$ curve in Fig. 3.1(a). Similarly, the demand for production loan can be obtained from (3.9) and, given other variables, its relationship with the rate of interest can be depicted as shown by the $\bar{P}F_{k2}/P_k$ curve in Fig. 3.1(b). Horizontally adding up the curves $i(\bar{P}C_1^l)$ and $\bar{P}F_{k2}/P_k$ and multiplying the sum by n, the market demand curve for loan, M, is obtained, and it is shown, as mapped against the rate of interest, by the curve i in Fig. 3.1(c) where M is measured along $00'$ with 0 as the origin and the rate of interest is measured along the vertical axis. Note that given the monopolistic position of the capitalist farm in the credit market, the aggregate demand curve for loan facing the capitalist farm has be to necessarily downward sloping. The curve i/θ is then obtained from this aggregate demand curve by using the average-marginal relationship.

The demand of the capitalist farm for $\bar{P}_k F_2$ can be derived from (3.23) and its relationship to the rate of interest is shown in terms of the curve $\bar{P}/\bar{P}_k F_{k2}$ in Fig. 3.1c, where $\bar{P}_k K_2$ is measured along $0'0$ with $0'$ as the origin and i is measured along the corresponding vertical axis. The length of $00'$ is equal to the total amount of wealth, $A_2(t)$, that the capitalist farm has chosen to hold in this period. From the intersection of the curves i/θ and $\bar{P}_k F_{k2}/\bar{P}_k$ in Fig. 3.1c, the equilibrium rate of interest is determined along with the allocation of A_2 between M and $\bar{P}_k F_{k2}/\bar{P}_k$ by the capitalist farm. Given this rate of interest, each family farm decides on the amounts of consumption loan and production loan it will take, as shown in Fig. 3.1(a, b). It is clear from (3.23) that for an interior solution to this problem of allocation between M and $\bar{P}_k F_{k2}/\bar{P}_k$ it is necessary to have $e > 1$. If $e \leq 1$, then the solution, as known from the standard theory of monopoly, tends to be in the neighbourhood of a corner with the capitalist farm trying to charge an infinitely high rate of interest for an infinitesimally small amount of loan. We are therefore led to distinguish between two possible situations:

1. The level of the average net income of the family farm is low and it is taking loans for both consumption and production, but the income is still above that level at which the family farm has to take consumption loan to meet the biologically minimum subsistence needs. In other words, the consumption needs can still be made flexible in the event of a sufficiently high rate of interest, implying thereby that $e \not< 1$ for the entire range of the aggregate curve for loan.
2. The other possibility is that the level of the average net income of the family farm is in fact so low that consumption loan is taken by the family farm for subsistence needs. Then the value of e may very well be below 1 over the entire range of the aggregate demand curve for loan[11] with the result that the capitalist farm can really charge a high enough rate of interest until the family farm becomes totally impoverished and is forced to sell his land and join the ranks of landless labour at a subsistence wage.[12] In this case, the solution is self-evident and we have nothing more to say about it by way of analysis, apart from men-

---

[11] This special situation is likely to arise particularly in the event of some unpredictable needs in consumption or production, and then the family farm can indeed find itself placed in a vulnerable position.

[12] The process cannot go beyond this point, because it is to the obvious interest of the capitalist farm to keep the family farmer alive in order to get the supply of labour.

tioning that this situation actually represents the terminal state of process relating to the behaviour of capital accumulation and the impoverishment of the family farm in a dualistic agriculture, and when the system comes to this state, then the complete impoverishment of the family farm becomes imminent.

We shall come back to this situation (2) later on. But it needs to be pointed out here, as was also mentioned once in Chapter 2, that the purpose of this chapter is not simply to describe this terminal state, although it may very well be the case with some of the present-day dualistic agriculture, but also to try to explain and understand the historical process by which a dualistic agriculture is actually brought to this terminal state, the tendencies which are inherent in this system and make it move in a particular direction. To be able to do that, it is important to start from a situation which is somewhat away from the terminal state, and therefore we choose the situation (1) as the description of the initial state and develop an analysis of the entire process of evolution from that point onward. It will be seen in the course of this analysis that the situation (2) will in fact come to appear as a part of that evolutionary process.

As an offshoot of this discussion, one can consider the value of $e(t)$ in any period t as directly related to the level of average net income available to the family farm in that period, that is, $y_1(t-1)$ and, since $\theta(t) = \dfrac{1}{1 - 1/e(t)}$, one can also write,

$$\theta(t) = \theta y_1(t-1), \text{ with } \frac{d\theta}{dy_1(t-1)} = \theta' < 0. \tag{3.28}$$

* * *

To sum up, given the objective of maximising the sum of discounted utility relating to per head consumption of the family members over a stipulated time horizon, the optimum decision rules for the family farms with respect to the relevant variables are given by (3.8′), (3.9), (3.11″), and those of the capitalist farm by (3.20), (3.23), and (3.26). These rules, taken together with the definitional equations, define the basic equational structure of our model of the dualistic agriculture for any particular period. For convenience of later reference, let us collect the equations in one place:

The Family Farm:

$$y_1(t) = \frac{\bar{P} F(\bar{T}_1, K_1(t), L_1(t)) + (w(t) - \mu) L_2(t)}{\bar{L}_1(t)} \quad (3.2')$$

$$- \frac{i(t) \bar{P}_k K_1(t) + (1 + i(t)) \bar{P} C_1^I(t)}{\bar{L}_1(t)}$$

$$L_1(t) + L_2(t) = \bar{L}_1(t) \quad (3.3)$$

$$\bar{P} F_{L1}(\bar{T}_1, K_1(t), L_1(t)) = w(t) - \mu \quad (3.8')$$

$$\frac{\bar{P}}{\bar{P}_k} F_{K1}(\bar{T}_1, K_1(t), L_1(t)) = i(t) \quad (3.9)$$

$$\bar{P} C_1^I(t) = \psi\left(i(t), w(t), y_1(t-1), \bar{L}_1(t); \mu, \lambda_1, g, B_1, B_2\right) \quad (3.11'')$$

The Capitalist Farm:

$$y_2(t) = \frac{\bar{P} F(\bar{T}_2, K_2(t), nL_2(t) - w(t) nL_2(t))}{\bar{L}_2(t)} + \frac{i(t) M(t)}{\bar{L}_2(t)} \quad (3.14)$$

$$M(t) = n\bar{P}_k K_1(t) + n\bar{P} C_1^I(t) \quad (3.13)$$

$$\bar{P} F_{L2}(\bar{T}_2, K_2(t), nL_2(t)) = w(t) \quad (3.20)$$

$$\theta\left(y_1(t-1) \frac{\bar{P}}{\bar{P}_k} F_{k2}\right)(\bar{T}_2, K_2(t), nL_2(t)) = i(t) \quad (3.23)$$

$$A_2(t) = \bar{P}_k K_2(t) + M(t) \equiv f\left(\frac{i(t)}{\theta(t)}, y_2(t-1), \bar{L}_2(t); \lambda_2, g, D_1, D_2\right) \quad (3.26)$$

Clearly, given B_1, B_2, D_1, D_2, g, θ, λ_1, and λ_2 as constants and $y_1(t-1)$, $y_2(t-1)$, $\bar{L}_1(t)$ and $\bar{L}_2(t)$ as parameters, we have, in any period t, as unknowns: $y_1(t)$, $K_1(t)$, $L_1(t)$, $w(t)$, $L_2(t)$, $i(t)$, $C_1^I(t)$, $K_2(t)$, $M(t)$, and $A_2(t)$, and the number of unknowns equals the number of equations. Another way of looking at this structure of equations is that, given the initial and the terminal condition as captured by the constants B_1, B_2, D_1, and D_2, and given other structural constants, g, μ, λ_1, and λ_2, the optimal time profiles of $\bar{P}C_1^l(t)$ and $A_2(t)$ and, associated with them, the profiles of all other variables are uniquely defined (except for the singular cases). The set of equations mentioned above is nothing but the characterisation of these profiles in a particular period of time, And, in this characterisation, the parameters clearly are $y_1(t-1), y_2(t-1), \bar{L}_1(t)$ and $\bar{L}_2(t)$; they change over time driving the system to the next period. To know the intertemporal behaviour of the system, which is the next step of our analysis, it is therefore essential to know the direction of changes in these four parameters.

It needs to be mentioned here that in finding out the qualitative nature of these parametric changes as well as deriving many other subsequent results, for the manoeuvrability of a differential operator, we shall work in terms of time derivatives rather than in terms of time differences. However, the underlying period analytic structure of our model, which was described in Chapter 2 and formalised in this chapter, will always be implied and, once the derivations are over, we shall interpret the results by coming back to this framework of period analysis.

With this in mind, our problem now is to find out the signs of the time derivatives of $\bar{L}_1, \bar{L}_2, y_1$ and y_2. Of these four parameters, the signs of $\bar{L}_1$ and $\bar{L}_2$ are already known to be positive by (3.4) and (3.15). The signs of the remaining two, dy_1/dt and dy_2/dt, will be given by the following propositions.

Proposition 1: Given the objective (3.18) if the rate of capital accumulation in the capitalist farm does not exceed the golden rule value, then $dy_2/dt \geq 0$, except for the case when the system is self-destructive.

Proof: Given the objective (3.18), it is clear from (3.21) that if

$$\frac{\bar{P}}{\bar{P}_k} F_{k2}\left(\bar{T}_2, K_2(t), nL_2(t)\right) \geq \lambda_2(1+g) \tag{3.29}$$

that is, if the rate of capital accumulation in the capitalist farm of the underdeveloped dualistic agriculture does not exceed the golden rule-catenary turnpike level (an assumption which can be made without straining any credibility, at least in the beginning of the process), then it follows from the concavity of U that

$$\Delta c_1(t) > 0 \tag{3.30}$$

The same result can be stated in continuous time with the objective (3.18) expressed as

$$\max \int_0^{T_2} e^{-\rho_2 t} U(c_2(t)) dt \qquad (3.18')$$

where ρ_2 is the rate of time preference of the capitalist farm and c_2 is to be written as

$$c_2 = \frac{y_2}{\bar{P}} - \frac{\bar{P}_k \frac{dK_2}{dt} + \frac{dM}{dt}}{\bar{P} \bar{L}_2} \qquad (3.16')$$

The continuous analogue of (3.21) is:

$$e^{-\rho_2 t} U' \left[\frac{F_{k2}}{\bar{L}_2} \right] = \frac{d}{dt} \left[e^{-\rho_2 t} U' \frac{\bar{P}_k}{\bar{P} \bar{L}_2} \right]$$

$$\text{or, } -\frac{dU'}{dt} / U' = \frac{\bar{P} F_{k2}}{\bar{P}_k} - (\rho_2 + g) \qquad (3.21')$$

which shows that if $\bar{P} F_{k2} / \bar{P}_k \geq \rho_2 + g$, the continuous counterpart of (3.29), then

$$\frac{dc_2}{dt} \geq 0, \text{ by the concavity of } U. \qquad (3.30')$$

Next, treating $A_2 (= \bar{P}_k K_2 + M)$ as one variable, we derive the corresponding Euler equation and then, multiplying both sides of the equation by dA_2/dt, express it in the following alternative form[13]:

$$\frac{d}{dt} \left[e^{-\rho_2 t} U + \frac{dA_2}{dt} e^{-\rho_2 t} U \right] = -\rho_2 e^{-\rho_2 t} U \qquad (3.31)$$

---

[13] See Gelfand, I.M. and Fomin, S.V., Calculus of Variations, Prentice-Hall (1963), pp. 18–19.

$$U'\frac{dc_2}{dt} + \frac{d^2A_2}{dt^2}\frac{U'}{\overline{PL}_2} - \frac{dA_2}{dt}\frac{U'g}{\overline{PL}_2} + \frac{dA_2}{dt}\frac{1}{\overline{PL}_2}\left[U''\frac{dc_2}{dt} - U'\rho_2\right] = 0 \quad (3.32)$$

We can now distinguish between the two cases depending on whether (1) $dA_2/dt \geq 0$ or, (2) $dA_2/dt < 0$.

Case 1: $dA_2/dt \geq 0$: In this case, given (3.30′) and the concavity of U, it follows from (3.32) that

$$\frac{dc_2}{dt} + \frac{d^2A}{dt^2}\frac{1}{\overline{PL}_2} - \frac{dA_2}{dt}\frac{g}{\overline{PL}_2} \geq 0 \quad (3.33)$$

which, by (3.16′), is equivalent to

$$\frac{dy_2}{dt} \geq 0. \quad (3.34)$$

Case 2: $dA_2/dt < 0$: Here, one can again have two possibilities: (1) the absolute value of $[U''Udc_2/dt - U'\rho_2]$ in (3.32) is not high enough so that (3.33) continues to hold and we have the same result as (3.34), or (2) the absolute value of $[U''dc_2/dt - U'P_2]$ is high enough to make

$$\frac{dc_2}{dt} + \frac{d^2A_2}{dt^2}\frac{1}{\overline{PL}_2} - \frac{dA_2}{dt}\frac{g}{\overline{PL}_2} < 0, \text{ or} \quad (3.33')$$

$$\frac{dy_2}{dt} < 0. \quad (3.34')$$

But, given, $dc_2/dt > 0$, this also means that $d^2A_2/dt^2 < 0$ along with $dA_2/dt < 0$, implying that the system is self-destructive over a finite time horizon.

Comment: Given the objective of maximising $\int_0^{T_2} e^{-\rho_2 t}U(c_2(t))dt$, the last situation, the possibility (2) under the case 2, is naturally ruled out if either the stipulated time horizon is considered to be sufficiently long or the terminal rate of growth of wealth is required not to fall below a certain positive number. Thus one can conclude that under quite general conditions, (3.18) can be taken to imply $dy_2/dt \geq 0$.

Proposition 2: Given the objective (3.6) and that the rate of capital accumulation in the family farm does not exceed the golden rule value, $dy_1/dt > 0$ if $d\bar{P}C_1^l / dt \leq 0$, and $dy_2/dt \leq 0$ implies $d\bar{P}C_1^l / dt > 0$.

Proof: Given the objective (3.6), it is clear from (3.10) that if

$$1 + i(t) \geq \lambda_1 (1 + g) \tag{3.35}$$

that is, noting from (3.9) that $i(t) = \bar{P}F_{k1}(\ )/\bar{P}_k$, if the rate of growth of capital accumulation in the family farm does not exceed the golden rule level, then

$$\Delta c_1(t) \geq 0. \tag{3.36}$$

Formulating the problem in continuous time, it can again be shown, exactly in the same way as in the proof of Proposition 1, that

$$\frac{dc_1}{dt} \geq 0 \quad \text{if} \ \frac{\bar{P}F_{k1}}{\bar{P}_k} > \rho_1 + g, \tag{3.36'}$$

where ρ_1 is the rate of time preference of the family farm and c_1 is to be written as:

$$c_1 = \frac{y_1}{\bar{P}} + \frac{C_1^l}{L_1} \tag{3.5'}$$

From this expression of c_1 it is immediate that

$$\frac{1}{\bar{P}} \frac{dy_1}{dt} = \frac{dc_1}{dt} - \frac{dC_1^l}{dt} \frac{1}{L_1} + g \frac{C_1^l}{L}, \tag{3.37}$$

so that by using (3.26) it follows that if $d\bar{P}C_1^l / dt \leq 0$, then $dy_1/dt > 0$, and $dy_1/dt \leq 0$ implies $d\bar{P}C_1^l / dt > 0$.

Proposition 3: If the weighted average of the rates of capital accumulation in the family and capitalist farms, weights being the rentals on capital used in the respective farms, is not high enough to exceed the rate of growth of labour force by an amount, defined by the rate of growth of

THE MODEL   33

labour force, the amount and the rate of change of the consumption loan and the shares of land and capital, then $dy_2/dt \geq 0$ implies $dy_1/dt < 0$, and $dy_1/dt \geq 0$ implies $dy_2/dt < 0$.

Proof: From (3.2) and (3.14) the expression of dy_1/dt and dy_2/dt can be derived as:

$$\frac{dy_1}{dt} = \frac{1}{\bar{L}_1}\left[\begin{array}{l}\bar{P}F_{K1}\dfrac{dK_1}{dt} + (w-\mu)g\bar{L}_1 + \dfrac{dw}{dt}L_2 \\ -\dfrac{d}{dt}\{i\bar{P}_K K_1 + (1+i)\bar{P}C_1^l\} - gY_1\end{array}\right], \text{ and} \quad (3.38)$$

$$\frac{dy_2}{dt} = \frac{1}{\bar{L}_2}\left[\bar{P}F_{K2}\frac{dk_2}{dt} - \frac{dw}{dt}nL_2 + \frac{d}{dt}(iM) - gY_2\right] \quad (3.39)$$

Now, quite generally, it is true that

$$gY_2 - \bar{P}F_{K2}\frac{dK_2}{dt} > n\left[\bar{P}F_{K1}\frac{dK_1}{dt} + (w-\mu)g\bar{L}_1 - \frac{d\bar{P}C_1^l}{dt} - gY_1\right]$$

$$\text{if } g\left[(n\bar{P}F_{k1}K_1 + \bar{P}F_{k2}K_2) + (n\bar{P}F_{T1}\bar{T}_1 + \bar{P}F_{T2}\bar{T}_2)\right] \quad (3.40)$$

$$+ n\frac{d\bar{P}C_1^l}{dt} > n\bar{P}F_{k1}\frac{dK_1}{dt} + \bar{P}F_{k2}\frac{dK_2}{dt}$$

(where $F_{Ti} = \partial F(\ )/\partial T_i|_{T_i=\bar{T}_i}$, $i = 1, 2$ and use has been made of $\mu > 0$ and the homogeneity property of F), that is, if,

$$g + \left[g\frac{n\bar{P}F_{T1}\bar{T}_1 + \bar{P}F_{T2}\bar{T}_2}{n\bar{P}F_{k1}K_1 + \bar{P}F_{k2}K_2} + \frac{\dfrac{d\bar{P}C_1}{dt}}{PC_1^l}\frac{n\bar{P}C_1^l}{n\bar{P}F_{k1}K_1 + \bar{P}F_{k2}K_2}\right] \quad (3.41)$$

$$> \frac{n\bar{P}F_{k1}K_1 G_{k1} + \bar{P}F_{k2}K_2 G_{k2}}{n\bar{P}F_{k1}K_1 + \bar{P}F_{k2}K_2},$$

where $G_{ki} = dK_i/dt/K_i$, $i = 1, 2$. Clearly, (3.41) is the statement of the condition that the weighted average of the rates of capital accumulation in the family and capitalist farms, weights being the rentals on capital used in the respective farms, does not exceed the rate of growth of labour force by an amount defined by the rate of growth of labour force, the rate of change in the consumption loan, and the ratio between the shares of land and capital, and that between the value of consumption loan and share of capital.

From (3.39) it is evident that $dy_2/dt \geq 0$ implies

$$\frac{d}{dt}(iM) \geq \frac{dw}{dt} nL_2 - \bar{P} F_{k2} \frac{dK_2}{dt} + gY_2 \qquad (3.42)$$

Now, if (3.41) holds, then by using (3.40) and (3.42), it further follows that

$$\frac{d}{dt}(iM) > n\left[\bar{P} F_{k1} \frac{dK_1}{dt} + (w-\mu)g\bar{L}_1 + \frac{dw}{dt} L_2 - gY_1\right] \qquad (3.43)$$

or, by transferring $d/dt\,(iM)$ on the R.H.S. and then dividing both sides by n, we have

$$\frac{dy_1}{dt} < 0. \qquad (3.44)$$

In a symmetric manner it can be proved that given (3.41), $dy_1/dt \geq 0$ implies $dy_2/dt < 0$.

Comment: We shall henceforth assume that the agricultural sector of a less developed economy, such as we are interested in, cannot, to begin with, accumulate at a rate so much faster than the rate of growth of labour force that (3.41) gets violated. Since in such an agriculture the share of land is generally more dominant than the share of capital on the amount of consumption loan, and the value of g is significantly high, this is indeed a reasonable assumption to make about the initial state of this agriculture.

The import of Proposition 3 is that in an underdeveloped dualistic agriculture when the rate of capital accumulation is not taking place at a sufficiently fast rate, it is not possible for the capitalist farm to have $dy_2/dt \geq 0$ and the family farm to have $dy_1/dt \geq 0$ at the same time. Only one of the two groups can make it. And, in a situation where, given the distribution of income, the capitalist farm enjoys a monopolistic position in the credit market, it has a prior advantage of choosing its plan of saving and accumulation of $A_2(t)$ in an optimal fashion (i.e., satisfying (3.26), so that i is made to change over time in a way that $d/dt\,(iM)$, the increase in earnings from loan, and $\bar{P}F_{k_2}dK_2/dt$, the increase in earnings from capital accumulation in its own farm, taken together becomes larger than $dw/dt\, nL_2 + gY_2$, implying by (3.39) that $dy_2/dt \geq 0$). The family farm, so long as it operates atomistically in the labour and in the credit market and therefore takes w and i as parameters, has no such prior advantage. It acts as a follower after the decision has been taken by the capitalist farm with respect to the savings plan. And, when such a decision is taken by the capitalist farm so that $dy_2/dt \geq 0$, and the situation is not one of a sufficiently fast rate of accumulation, then, as shown in Proposition 3, the family farm ends up with $dy_1/dt < 0$. We are thus led to this following proposition:

Proposition 4: Given the bias in the distribution of income in favour of the capitalist farm and its consequent monopolistic position in the credit market, it has the advantage over the family farm in ensuring $dy_2/dt \geq 0$, and as the rate of capital accumulation to begin with satisfies (3.41), this implies, by Proposition 3, that $dy_1/dt < 0$.

With the signs of dy_1/dt and dy_2/dt thus known,[14] and the signs of $d\bar{L}_1/dt$ and $d\bar{L}_2/dt$ already given, we shall now proceed to derive, by totally differentiating the system of equations with respect to time, the qualitative properties of the time derivatives of all the relevant variables, and then, by analysing these derivatives, conclude about the intertemporal behaviour of the system.

---

[14] As pointed out at the end of Chapter 2, most of the decision rules of the family and the capitalist farms as well as the signs of the time derivations of the parameters could have been derived from a simpler specification of the objective, where both the farms are trying to maximise their respective net income (i.e., profit) in any period with an additional intertemporal requirement that this net income of any period should not fall below that of the last period. In the case of the family farm, for example, the maximisation of y_1 subject to (3.5) with a given value of c_1 yields the decision rules with respect to the use of L_1 and K_1 which are the same as (3.8) and (3.9). Similarly, for the capitalist farm, the maximisation of y_2 subject to (3.7) with a given value of A_2 gives the decision rules with respect to the use of L_2 and the allocation of A_2 between M and $\bar{P}_k K_2$ which are again the same as (3.20) and (3.23). The only problem about this kind of specification of the objective function, however, is connected with the derivation of the demand function for PC_1^l Consumption loan and A_2. The question of the demand function for PC_1^l can still be settled at least in our case, by specifying the level of per head consumption, c_1, to some predetermined minimum level, although that is not always the best way of explaining the consumption decision. But the problem is more serious with respect to the determination of the capitalist farm's decision on A_2. Furthermore it needs to be written that, with an open-ended specification of the intertemporal objective, such as $dy_2/dt \geq 0$ the decision on A also gets characterised by inequality and thus remains somewhat ill defined. And, to dodge the issue by saying that A_2 is a certain fixed proportion of, say, y_2 is not really explaining an important dimension of the choice problem of the capitalist farm with respect to A_2. This choice problem can be analysed only in terms of the type of specification of the objective function such as we have been working with.

At this point, a comment on methodology seems pertinent. In following this method of solution, what we are doing, in effect, is that we are observing the equations of motion of the system over a short range and, from such an observation of the "local" qualitative character of system over a short range and, from such an observation of the "local" qualitative character of the phase space, inferring about the "global" tendencies of the system. We are deliberately choosing this method as against the usual method of global phase construction, because if the system is known to have sufficient monotonicity, this is indeed a valid and at the same time a simpler substitute for the global technique. And, in the case of our model, we shall see that, because of the nature of the time functions of $y_1, y_2, \bar{L}_1$, and $\bar{L}_2$, there exists enough monotonicity in the system to warrant such a global qualitative inference from a local analysis.

References

Bhagwati, J., & Chakravarty, S. (1969). Contribution to Indian Economic Analysis. *American Economic Review, 59*, 1–73.

Gelfand, I. M., & Fomin, S. V. (1963). *Calculus of Variations* (pp. 18–19). New Jersey: Prentice-Hall.

Lewis, A. (1954). Economic Development with Unlimited Supplies of Labour. *Manchester School of Economics and Social Studies, 22*, 139–191.

Ramsey, F. (1928). A Mathematical Theory of Saving. *Economic Journal, 38*(152), 543–559.

Samuelson, P. A. A Turnpike Refutation of the Golden Rule of Welfare-Maximising Many-Year Plan. In R. C. Metron (Ed.), *The Collected Scientific Papers of Paul A. Samuelson* (Vol. 3, pp. 108–110). Cambridge, MA: MIT Press.

Sen, A. K. (1966). Peasants and Dualism with or Without Surplus Labour. *Journal of Political Economy, 74*, 425–450.

Stiglitz, J. E. (1969). Rural-Urban Migration, Surplus Labour and Relationship Between Urban and Rural Wages. *East African Economic Review, 12*, 58–67.

Stiglitz, J. E. (1974). Wage Determination and Unemployment in L.D.C.s. *Quarterly Journal of Economics, 88*, 194–227.

Visaria, P. (1970). *The Farmers, Preference for Work on Family Farms.* Report of the Committee of Experts on Unemployment Estimates, Government of India.

CHAPTER 4

Behaviour of the System over Time

Abstract In this chapter, the model as developed in the last section, is now used to analyse the special problem of capital accumulation is this agriculture. It is found that given an unequal distribution of income and wealth, and related imperfection of credit market, such agriculture can show a tendency to approach a state of zero rate of capital accumulation under certain plausible conditions, and this can be accompanied by a process of immiseration of family farms.

Keywords Zero rate of capital accumulation • Immiseration of family farms

From the standpoint of intertemporal analysis, the equations of the model, mentioned in the last chapter, can be further condensed as

$$F_{L1}[T_1, K_1(t), L_1(t)] + \frac{\mu}{P} = F_{L2}[\overline{T}_2, K_2(t), nL_2(t)] = \frac{w}{P} \quad (4.1)$$

$$L_1(t) + L_2(t) = \overline{L}_1(t) \quad (3.3)$$

$$\overline{PC}_1^I(t) = \psi\left[i(t), w(t), y_1(t-1), \overline{L}_1(t); \mu, \lambda_1, g, G_1, B_2\right] \quad (3.11)$$

$$\psi_1 < 0, \psi_2 > 0, \psi_3 < 0, \psi_4 > 0.$$

© The Author(s) 2018
A. K. Dasgupta, *Income Distribution, Market Imperfections and Capital Accumulation in a Developing Economy*,
https://doi.org/10.1007/978-981-13-1633-3_4

$$F_{K1}\left[\overline{T_1}, K_1(t), L_1(t)\right] = \theta(t) F_{K2}\left[\overline{T_2}, K_2(t), nL_2(t)\right] = i\frac{\overline{P_k}}{\overline{P}} \qquad (4.2)$$

$$A_2(t) = f\left[\frac{i(t)}{\theta(t)}, y_2(t-1), L_2(t); \lambda_2, g, D_1, D_2\right]$$
$$\equiv n\overline{P}C'_l(t) + n\overline{P_k}K_1(t) + \overline{P_k}K_2(t), \qquad (3.36)$$
$$f_1 > 0, f_2 > 0, f_3 > 0.$$

In calculating the changes of the variables over time, for reasons of convenience of working with time derivatives as mentioned before, we shall continue to work in the framework of continuous time, although the underlying period analytic structure should again be kept in mind, and we shall refer back to it for purposes of interpreting the results. For simplifying calculations, in the beginning we shall also hold θ constant and relax it later on. Now, totally differentiating those five equations with respect to time, and then eliminating di/dt and dw/dt, we get

$$\frac{\partial F_{L1}}{\partial K_1}\frac{dK_1}{dt} - \frac{\partial F_{L2}}{\partial K_2}\frac{dK_2}{dt} + \left(\frac{\partial F_{L1}}{\partial L_1} + n\frac{\partial F_{L2}}{\partial nL_2}\right) = n\frac{\partial F_{L2}}{\partial nL_2}\frac{\partial \overline{L_1}}{dt} \qquad (4.3)$$

$$\frac{\partial F_{k1}}{\partial K_1}\frac{dK_1}{dt} - \theta\frac{\partial F_{k2}}{\partial K_2}\frac{dK_2}{dt} + \left(\frac{\partial F_{k1}}{\partial L_1} + n\theta\frac{\partial F_{k2}}{\partial nL_2}\right)\frac{\partial L_1}{dt} = n\theta\frac{\partial F_{k2}}{\partial nL_2}\frac{\partial \overline{L_1}}{dt} \qquad (4.4)$$

$$\left\{\left(n\psi_1 - \frac{f_1}{\theta}\right)\frac{\overline{P}}{\overline{P_k}}\frac{\partial F_{k1}}{\partial K_1} + n\psi_2\frac{\partial F_{L1}}{\partial K_1} + n\overline{P_k}\right\}\frac{dk_1}{dt} + \overline{P_k}\frac{dk_2}{dt} \qquad (4.5)$$

$$+\left\{\left(n\psi_1 - \frac{f_1}{\theta}\right)\frac{\overline{P}}{\overline{P_k}}\frac{\partial F_{k1}}{\partial L_1} + n\psi_2 \overline{P}\frac{\partial F_{L1}}{\partial L_1}\right\}\frac{\partial L_1}{dt} = \frac{dx}{dt},$$

where

$$\frac{dx}{dt} = f_2\frac{dy_2}{dt} + f_3\frac{d\overline{L_2}}{dt} - n\psi_3\frac{dy_1}{dt} - n\psi_4\frac{d\overline{L_1}}{dt}. \qquad (4.6)$$

The Jacobian:

$$\Delta = \begin{vmatrix} \dfrac{\partial F_{L1}}{\partial K_1} & & n\dfrac{\partial F_{L2}}{\partial L_2} & \left(\dfrac{\partial F_{L1}}{\partial L_1} + n\dfrac{\partial F_{L2}}{\partial nL_2}\right) \\[6pt] \dfrac{\partial F_{k1}}{\partial K_1} & & -\theta\dfrac{\partial F_{L2}}{\partial K_2} & \left(\dfrac{\partial F_{k1}}{\partial L_1} + n\theta\dfrac{\partial F_{k2}}{\partial nL_2}\right) \\[8pt] \left(n\psi_1 - \dfrac{f_1}{\theta}\right)\dfrac{\bar{P}}{\bar{P}_k}\dfrac{\partial F_{k1}}{\partial K_1} + n\psi_1 \dfrac{\partial F_{L1}}{\partial K_1} + n\bar{P}_k & P_k & & \left(n\psi_1 - \dfrac{f_1}{\theta}\right)\dfrac{\bar{P}}{\bar{P}_k}\dfrac{\partial F_{k1}}{\partial L_1} \\[6pt] & & & + n\psi_2 \bar{P}\dfrac{\partial F_{k1}}{\partial L_1} \end{vmatrix}$$

$$= \left\{ \bar{P}_k + \theta\left(n\psi_1 - \dfrac{f_1}{\theta}\right)\dfrac{\bar{P}}{\bar{P}_k}\dfrac{\partial Fk_2}{\partial k_2} + n\psi_2 \bar{P}\dfrac{\partial F_{L2}}{\partial k_2}\right\}\left\{\dfrac{\partial F_{K1}}{\partial k_1}\dfrac{\partial F_{L1}}{\partial L_1} - \dfrac{\partial F_{K1}}{\partial L_1}\dfrac{\partial F_{L1}}{\partial k_1}\right\}$$

$$+ \theta n^2 \{\bar{P}k + \dfrac{1}{n}\left(n\psi_1 - \dfrac{f_1}{\theta}\right) + \psi_2 \bar{P}\dfrac{\partial F_{L1}}{\partial k_1}\}\left\{\dfrac{\partial F_{k2}}{\partial k_2}\dfrac{\partial F_{L2}}{\partial nL_2} - \dfrac{\partial F_{L2}}{\partial nL_2}\dfrac{\partial F_{k2}}{\partial nL_2} - \dfrac{\partial F_{L2}}{\partial k_2}\right\}$$

$$+ n\bar{P}_k \left\{\dfrac{\partial Fk_1}{\partial k_1}\dfrac{\partial FL_2}{\partial nL_2} - \dfrac{\partial Fk_1}{\partial L_1}\dfrac{\partial FL_2}{\partial k_2}\right\} + \theta n\bar{P}_k \left\{\dfrac{\partial F_{L1}}{\partial L_1}\dfrac{\partial F_{k2}}{\partial k_2} - \dfrac{\partial F_{L1}}{\partial k_1}\dfrac{\partial F_{k2}}{\partial nL_2}\right\},$$

by grouping the term appropriately. On inspecting this expression, it follows that

$$\Delta > 0, \tag{4.7}$$

given the usual properties of the partial derivations of neoclassical production function, the signs of the partial derivatives of the functions ψ and f, the second-order conditions of maximum of (3.6) and (3.18), and assuming that the forces of diminishing returns are stronger than those of complementarity; that is,

$$\left|\dfrac{\partial F_{ki}}{\partial k_k}\right| > \left|\dfrac{\partial F_{ki}}{\partial K_i}\right| \text{ etc.}$$

Using Cramer's rule, we then have

$$\frac{\partial K_1}{dt} = \frac{1}{\Delta} \begin{vmatrix} n\frac{\partial F_{L2}}{\partial nL_2}\frac{d\bar{L}_1}{dt} & -\frac{\partial F_{L2}}{\partial K_2} & \left(\frac{\partial F_{L1}}{\partial L_1} + \frac{\partial F_{L2}}{\partial nL_2}\right) \\ n\theta\frac{\partial F_{K2}}{\partial nL_2}\frac{d\bar{L}_1}{dt} & -\theta\frac{\partial F_{K2}}{\partial K_2} & \left(\frac{\partial F_{k1}}{\partial L_1} + n\frac{\partial F_{k2}}{\partial nL_2}\right) \\ \frac{dx}{dt} & \bar{P}_k & \left(n\psi_1 - \frac{f_1}{\theta}\right)\frac{\bar{P}}{\bar{P}_k}\frac{\partial F_{k1}}{\partial L_1} + n\psi_2\bar{P}\frac{\partial F_{L1}}{\partial L_1} \end{vmatrix} \quad (4.8)$$

$$= \frac{1}{\Delta}\left[n\theta\left\{\frac{dx}{dt} - \left(n\psi_1 - \frac{f_1}{\theta}\right)\frac{\bar{P}}{\bar{P}_k}\frac{\partial F_{k1}}{\partial L_1}\frac{d\bar{L}_1}{dt} - n\psi_2\bar{P}\frac{\partial F_{L1}}{\partial L_1}\frac{d\bar{L}_1}{dt}\right\}\left\{\frac{\partial F_{K2}}{\partial K_2}\frac{\partial F_{L2}}{\partial L_2} - \frac{\partial F_{K2}}{\partial nL_2}\frac{\partial F_{L2}}{\partial K_2}\right\}\right.$$

$$\left. + \frac{dx}{dt}\left\{\theta\frac{\partial F_{L1}}{\partial L_1}\frac{\partial F_{k2}}{\partial k_2} - \frac{\partial F_{k1}}{\partial L_1}\frac{\partial F_{L2}}{\partial K_2}\right\} + n\bar{P}_k\frac{d\bar{L}_1}{dt}\left\{\theta\frac{\partial F_{L1}}{\partial L_1}\frac{\partial F_{k2}}{\partial nL_2} - \frac{\partial F_{k1}}{\partial L_1}\frac{\partial F_{L2}}{\partial nL_2}\right\}\right]$$

and

$$\frac{dk_2}{dt} = \frac{1}{\Delta}\begin{vmatrix} \frac{\partial F_{L1}}{\partial K_1} & n\frac{\partial F_{L2}}{\partial nL_2}\frac{d\bar{L}1}{dt} & \left(\frac{\partial F_{L1}}{\partial L_1} + n\frac{\partial F_{L2}}{\partial nL_2}\right) \\ \frac{\partial F_{k1}}{\partial k_1} & n\theta\frac{\partial F_{k2}}{\partial nL_2}\frac{d\bar{L}_1}{dt} & \left(\frac{\partial F_{K1}}{\partial L_1} + n\theta\frac{\partial F_{k2}}{\partial nL_2}\right) \\ \left(n\psi_1 - \frac{f_1}{\theta}\right)\frac{\bar{P}}{\bar{p}_k}\frac{\partial F_{k1}}{\partial k_1} + n\psi_2\bar{P}\frac{\partial F_{L1}}{\partial k_1} + n\bar{P}_k\frac{dx}{dt} & & \left(n\psi_1 - \frac{f_1}{\theta}\right)\frac{\bar{P}}{\bar{P}_k}\frac{\partial F_{k1}}{\partial L_1} \\ & & + n\psi_2\bar{P}\frac{\partial F_{L1}}{\partial F_1} \end{vmatrix}$$

(4.9)

$$= \frac{1}{\Delta}\left[\left\{\frac{dx}{dt} - \theta n\left(n\psi_1 - \frac{f_1}{\theta}\right)\frac{\bar{P}}{\bar{P}_k}\frac{\partial F_{k2}}{\partial nL_2}\frac{d\bar{L}_1}{dt} - n^2\psi_2\bar{P}\frac{\partial F_{L2}}{\partial nL_2}\frac{\partial \bar{L}_1}{dt}\right\}\left\{\frac{\partial F_{k1}}{\partial K_1}\frac{\partial F_{L1}}{\partial L_1} - \frac{\partial F_{k1}}{\partial L_1}\frac{\partial F_{L1}}{\partial K_1}\right\}\right.$$

$$\left. + n\frac{dx}{dt}\left\{\frac{\partial F_{k1}}{\partial K_1}\frac{\partial F_{L2}}{\partial nL_2} - \theta\frac{\partial F_{L1}}{\partial K_1}\frac{\partial F_{K2}}{\partial nL_2}\right\} + n^2\bar{P}\frac{d\bar{L}_1}{dt}\left\{\frac{\partial F_{k1}}{\partial L_1}\frac{\partial F_{L2}}{\partial nL_2} - \frac{\partial F_{L1}}{\partial L_1}\frac{\partial F_{k2}}{\partial nL_2}\right\}\right]$$

Hence, the aggregate capital accumulation of this dualistic agriculture can be expressed as:

$$n\frac{dK_1}{dt}+\frac{dK_2}{dt}=\frac{1}{\Delta}\left[n^2\theta\left\{\begin{array}{l}\frac{dx}{dt}-\left(n\psi_1-\frac{f_1}{\theta}\right)\frac{\overline{P}}{\overline{P}_k}\frac{\partial F_{k1}}{\partial L_1}\frac{\partial L_1}{\partial \overline{L}_1}\frac{d\overline{L}_1}{dt}\\ -n\psi_2\overline{P}\frac{\partial F_{L1}}{\partial L_1}\frac{\partial L_1}{\partial \overline{L}_1}\frac{d\overline{L}_1}{dt}\end{array}\right\}\right.$$

$$\left\{\frac{\partial F_{k2}}{\partial K_2}\frac{\partial F_{L2}}{\partial L_2}-\frac{\partial F_{k2}}{\partial L_2}\frac{\partial F_{L2}}{\partial K_2}\right\}+\left\{\begin{array}{l}\frac{dx}{dt}-\theta\left(n\psi_1-\frac{f_1}{\theta}\right)\frac{\overline{P}}{\overline{P}_k}\frac{\partial F_{k2}}{\partial nL_2}\frac{\partial nL_2}{\partial L_2}\frac{\partial \overline{L}_1}{dt}\\ -n\psi_2\overline{P}\frac{\partial F_{L2}}{\partial nL_2}\frac{\partial nL_2}{\partial \overline{L}_1}\frac{d\overline{L}_1}{dt}\end{array}\right\} \quad (4.10)$$

$$\left\{\frac{\partial F_{k1}}{\partial K_1}\frac{\partial F_{L1}}{\partial L_1}-\frac{\partial F_{k1}}{\partial L_1}\frac{\partial F_{L1}}{\partial K_1}\right\}+n\frac{dx}{dt}\left\{\begin{array}{l}\theta\left(\frac{\partial F_{L1}}{\partial L_1}\frac{\partial F_{k2}}{\partial K_2}-\frac{\partial F_{L1}}{\partial K_1}\frac{\partial F_{k2}}{\partial nL_2}\right)\\ +\left(\frac{\partial F_{K1}}{\partial K_1}\frac{\partial F_{L2}}{\partial nL_2}-\frac{\partial F_{k1}}{\partial L_1}\frac{\partial F_{L2}}{\partial K_2}\right)\end{array}\right\}\right],$$

using $L_1+L_2=\overline{L}_1$.

Given, again, the second-order conditions of maximum and that the forces of diminishing returns are stronger than those of complementarity, it follows by using (4.1) and (4.2) that

$$n\frac{dk_1}{dt}+\frac{dk_2}{dt}<0 \text{ if}$$

$$\frac{dx}{dt}-n\psi_1\frac{\partial i}{\partial \overline{L}_1}\frac{d\overline{L}_1}{dt}+\frac{f_1}{\theta}\frac{\partial i}{\partial \overline{L}_1}\frac{d\overline{L}_1}{dt}-n\psi_2\frac{\partial w}{\partial \overline{L}_1}\frac{d\overline{L}_1}{dt}<0 \quad (4.11)$$

which obviously also implies

$$\frac{dx}{dt}<0 \quad (4.12)$$

By using the definition of dx/dt, given by (4.6), the condition (4.11) can be written as

$$\frac{f_1}{\theta}\frac{\partial i}{\partial \overline{L}_1}+f_2\frac{dy_2}{dt}+f_3\frac{d\overline{L}_2}{dt}<n\left[\psi_1\frac{\partial i}{\partial \overline{L}_1}\frac{d\overline{L}_1}{dt}+\psi_2\frac{\partial w}{\partial \overline{L}_1}\frac{d\overline{L}_1}{dt}+\psi_3\frac{dy_1}{dt}+\psi_4\frac{d\overline{L}_1}{dt}\right] \quad (4.13)$$

It is clear from (3.11″) and (3.36) that the L.H.S. of (4.13) shows nothing but the total change in A_2 over time following the changes in the relevant parameters and the R.H.S. the total change in $\bar{P}C_1^I$ of all the family farms taken together following similar changes in its relevant parameters.

So long, for the sake of simplification, θ has been held constant. It is known, however, from (3.28) that $\theta = \theta(y_1)$ with $d\theta/dy_1 < 0$ and accordingly θ is expected to change over time due to change in y_1. It is appropriate now to incorporate this change into our analysis.

There will be essentially two additional changes in the system following this variation in θ.

1. There will be a change in i/θ and, through that, an additional variation in A_2, to be captured by $f_1[\partial(i/\theta)/\partial\theta](\partial\theta/\partial y_1)(dy_1/dt)$. It needs to be pointed out that change in i/θ is inversely related with θ. To see this, consider a situation where θ has fallen, and, for convenience of illustration, consider it where θ has fallen all the way to the value 1; that is, the interest elasticity of the aggregate demand for Loan, M, has increased to infinity, implying thereby a change from imperfect to perfect credit market.[1]

Then, referring to Fig. 4.1, it is clear that as θ falls to the value 1 and the i/θ becomes horizontal at i_1, the system moves from its old equilibrium E_0 to the new equilibrium E_1 and the value of i/θ increases from $E_0 H_0$ to $E_1 M_1$. It should be noted here that although the value of i/θ increases, and the inverse relationship between θ and i/θ is thus demonstrated, the value of i actually falls from i_0 in the old equilibrium to i_1 in the new equilibrium.

2. This variation in i, consequent upon a change in θ, will now produce the second change in the system by generating an additional variation in $\bar{P}C_1^I$. This can be expressed as $\psi_1(\partial i/\partial\theta)(\partial\theta/\partial y_1)(dy_1/dt)$, where $(\partial i/\partial\theta) > 0$.

Accommodating these two changes, in A_2 and $\bar{P}C_1^I$ caused by the change in θ, the condition (4.13) can be generalised as

---

[1] This case will come to be very relevant for our discussion in Chapter 5.

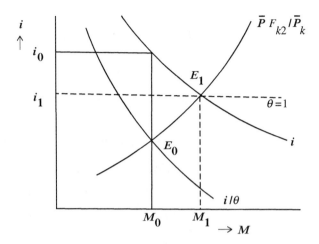

Fig. 4.1 Shift in equilibrium

$$f_1 \frac{\partial\left(\frac{i}{\theta}\right)}{\partial \bar{L}_1} \frac{d\bar{L}_1}{dt} + f_1 \frac{\partial\left(\frac{i}{\theta}\right)}{\partial \theta} \frac{\partial \theta}{\partial y_1} \frac{dy_1}{dt} + f_2 \frac{dy_2}{dt} + f_3 \frac{d\bar{L}_2}{dt}$$
$$< n\left[\psi_1 \frac{\partial i}{\partial \bar{L}_1} \frac{d\bar{L}_1}{dt} + \psi_1 \frac{\partial i}{\partial \theta} \frac{\partial \theta}{\partial y_1} \frac{dy_1}{dt} + \psi_2 \frac{\partial w}{\partial \bar{L}_1} \frac{d\bar{L}_1}{dt} + \psi_3 \frac{dy_1}{dt} + \psi_4 \frac{d\bar{L}_1}{dt} \right] \quad (4.14)$$

With a little effort, this condition can also be expressed in an alternative way, in terms of the elasticities of the relevant variables:

$$A_2\left[e_{f,\frac{i}{\theta}} e_{\frac{i}{\theta},\bar{L}_1} g + e_{f,\frac{i}{\theta}} e_{\frac{i}{\theta},\theta} e_{\theta,y_1} \frac{dy_1}{dt}/y_1 + e_{f,y_2} \frac{dy_2}{dt}/y_2 + e_{f,\bar{L}_2} g \right]$$
$$< n\bar{P}C_1^l\left[-e_{\psi,i} e_{i,\bar{L}_1} g + e_{\psi,i} e_{i,\theta} e_{\theta,y_1} \frac{dy_1}{dt}/y_1 - e_{\psi,w} e_{w,\bar{L}_1} g - e_{\psi,y} \frac{dy_1}{dt}/y_1 + e_{\psi} \bar{L} y \right] \quad (4.15)$$

where $e_{f,\frac{i}{\theta}} = \frac{\partial A_2}{\partial \frac{i}{\theta}} \frac{i}{A_2}$, $e_{f,y2} = (\partial A_2/\partial y_2)(y_2/A_2)$ and $e_{f,\bar{L}_2} = (\partial A_2/\partial \bar{L}_2)(\bar{L}_2/A_2)$ are the elasticities of A_2 with respect to $i/\theta, y_2$ and $\bar{L}_2$, $e_{\psi,i} = (\partial \bar{P}C_1^l/\partial i)(i/\bar{P}C_1^l)$,

$e_{\psi,w} = \left(\partial \bar{P} C_1^l / \partial w\right)\left(w / \bar{P} C_1^l\right)$, $e_{\psi,y1} = -\left(\partial \bar{P} C_1^l / \partial y_1\right)\left(y_1 / \partial \bar{P} C_1^l\right)$ and $e_{\psi,\bar{L}1} = -\left(\partial \bar{P} C_1^l / \partial \bar{L}_1\right)$ $\left(\bar{L}_1 / \bar{P} C_1^l\right)$ are the elasticities of $\bar{P}_2 C_1^l$ with respect to i, w, y_1 and

$\bar{L}_1, e_{\frac{i}{\theta}, \bar{L}_1} = \dfrac{\partial \frac{i}{\theta} \bar{L}_1}{\partial \bar{L}_1 \frac{i}{\theta}}$ and $e_{i/\theta,\theta} = \dfrac{\partial \frac{i}{\theta} \theta}{\partial \theta \frac{i}{\theta}}$ are the elasticities of i/θ with respect to

$\bar{L}_1$ and $\theta e_{i,\bar{L}_1} = \left(\partial i / \partial \bar{L}_1\right) \cdot \left(\bar{L}_1 / i\right)$ and $e_{i,\theta} = \left(\partial i / \partial \theta\right)\left(\theta / i\right)$ are the elasticities of i with respect to $\bar{L}_1$ and θ, and finally, $e_{\theta,y_1} = -\left(\partial \theta / \partial y_1\right) \cdot \left(y_1 / \theta\right)$ and $e_{w,\bar{L}_1} = -\left(\partial w / \partial \bar{L}_1\right) \cdot \left(\bar{L}_1 / w\right)$ are the elasticity of θ with respect to y_1 and that of w with respect to $\bar{L}$, respectively. All these elasticities are defined, as usual, in terms of their absolute magnitudes.

Now, for the purpose of final interpretation, we like to express this condition, (4.14) or (4.15), by going back, as suggested at the outset, to our original framework of period analysis. Then, (4.14), for example, will have to be written as

$$f_1 = -\dfrac{\partial\left(\frac{i}{\theta}\right)}{\partial \bar{L}_1}\Delta \bar{L}_1(t) + f_1 \dfrac{\partial\left(\frac{i}{\theta}\right)}{\partial \theta}\dfrac{d\theta}{dy_1}\Delta y_1(t-1) + f_2 \Delta y_2(t-1) + f_3 \Delta \bar{L}_2(t) \quad (4.14')$$

$$< n\left[\psi_1 \dfrac{\partial i}{\partial \bar{L}_1}\Delta \bar{L}_1(t) + \psi_1 \dfrac{\partial i}{\partial \theta}\dfrac{d\theta}{dy_1}\Delta y_1(t-1) + \psi_2 \dfrac{\partial w}{\partial \bar{L}_1}\Delta \bar{L}_1(t) \right. \\ \left. + \psi_3 \Delta y_1(t-1) + \psi_4 \Delta \bar{L}_1(t)\right]$$

where all the partial derivatives, by the mean value theorem, are to be considered as evaluated at some interior points of the relevant intervals. In a similar way, (4.15) will be expressed as

$$A_2(t)\left[e_{f,\frac{i}{\theta}}e_{\frac{i}{\theta},\bar{L}_1}g + e_{f,\frac{i}{\theta}}e_{\frac{i}{\theta},\theta}e_{\theta,y_1}\dfrac{\Delta y_1(t-1)}{y_1(t-1)} + e_{f,y_2}\dfrac{\Delta y_2(t-1)}{y_2(t-1)} + e_{f,\bar{L}_2}g\right] \quad (4.15')$$

$$< n\bar{P} C_1^l(t)\left[-e_{\psi,i}e_{i,\bar{L}_1}g + e_{\psi,i}e_{i,\theta}e_{\theta,y_1}\dfrac{\Delta y_1(t-1)}{y_1(t-1)} - e_{\Psi,w}e_{w,\bar{L}_1}g - e_{\psi,y_1}\dfrac{\Delta y_1(t-1)}{y_1(t-1)} + e_{\psi,\bar{L}_1}g\right],$$

where all the elasticities are to be considered as arc, rather than point, elasticities.

This condition, (4.14′) or (4.15′), can now be interpreted in the following way. There are, as we know, four parameters, $\bar{L}_1(t), \bar{L}_2(t), y_1(t-1)$, and $y_2(t-1)$, the changes in which make the system move. The directions of changes in these parameters are also known to us: $\bar{L}_1(t), \bar{L}_2(t)$, and $y_2(t-1)$ increase, while $y_1(t-1)$ falls, over time. As all of these parameters change at the same time, and in these directions, they produce a combined effect on each variable of the system. The condition (4.14′) is nothing but a description and a comparison of such combined effects or total changes in two crucial variables, the wealth of the capitalist farm, $A_2(t)$, and the aggregate consumption loan of all the family farms, $n\bar{P}C_1^l$. It is important to focus one's attention, among others, on these two variables, because by looking at their changes it is possible to conclude about the direction of aggregate capital accumulation.

Consider, first, the L.H.S. of (4.14′). It shows the total change in $A_2(t)$ when all the parameters are changing. An increase in $\bar{L}_1(t)$, going through the complementarity between $K_1(t)$, and between $K_2(t)$ and $nL_2(t)$, increases the value of $i(t)$ and therefore also of $[i(t)/\theta(t)]$, and with $f_1 > 0$ that increases $A_2(t)$ (the first term). On the other hand, as $y_1(t-1)$ falls over time, the value of $\theta_1(t)$ increases and, therefore, for reasons already considered, the value of $[i(t)/\theta(t)]$, falls, producing a dampening effect on $A_2(t)$ (the second term). Then, the third and fourth terms of the L.H.S. show the positive effect on $A_2(t)$ of the change in $y_2(t-1)$ and $\bar{L}_2(t)$, respectively.

The R.H.S. of (4.14′) shows the total change in $\bar{P}C_1^l(t)$ due to the variations in all the relevant parameters. Such parameters for $\bar{P}C_1^l(t)$ are $\bar{L}_1(t)$ and $y_1(t-1)$. The increase in $\bar{L}_1(t)$ affects $\bar{P}C_1^l(t)$ in three different ways: (a) by going through the complementarity between capital and labour and increasing thereby the value of $i(t)$, it tends to lower $\bar{P}C_1^l$ (the first term); (b) by reducing the value of $w(t)$ because of diminishing returns, it tends to reduce $\bar{P}C_1^l(t)$ (the third term); and finally (c) by itself, given that $\psi_4 > 0$, it increases $\bar{P}C_1^l(t)$ (the last term). The fall in $y_1(t-1)$, the other parameter, affects $\bar{P}C_1^l(t)$ in two opposite directions. On the one hand, such a fall is known to increase the demand for consumption loan (the fourth term); on the other, because of a consequent increase in $\theta(t)$ and $i(t)$, a reduction in $\bar{P}C_1^l(t)$ is also expected (the second term). Adding up all these, we get the R.H.S. of (4.14′) the net total change in $\bar{P}C_1^l(t)$.

Now, (4.14′), or its equivalent formulation in terms of elasticities, (4.15′), describes a special situation where the elasticities of f and ψ with respect to the relevant variables are such that, following a simultaneous change in all the parameters, the total increase in $\bar{P}C_1^I(t)$ is greater than the total increase $A_2(t)$. But, since $\Delta A_2(t) - n\Delta \bar{P}C_1^I(t) = n\Delta P_k K_1(t) + \Delta \bar{P}_k K_2(t)$, that immediately means that in such a situation the total capital accumulation in agriculture will be negative. Referring back to the Fig. 3.1(a–c), this situation will be depicted by the $i\left(\bar{P}C_1^I\right)$ curve in Fig. 3.1(a) shifting at a rate faster than the rate of expansion of the length 00′ in Fig. 3.1(c), forcing thereby a shrinking back of the demand curve for $\bar{P}_k K_1$ (of all the family farms) and $\bar{P}_k K_2$ taken together.

The purpose of emphasising this particular condition, this apparently special situation, is really to draw attention to an important, and a very generally plausible, tendency of the path of capital accumulation in a dualistic agriculture. For this type of agriculture, we have seen that the initial state can be taken to be characterised as one where the average income of the family farm is very low and, relative to that, the average income of the capitalist farm is significantly high. Given this distribution of income, the income elasticity of the family farm's demand for $\bar{P}C_1^I$ is likely to be much higher than its interest elasticity, and then the gap between these elasticities, $\left(e_{\psi,y_1} - e_{\psi,i}\right)$ is also likely to be much wider than the gap between the corresponding elasticities, $\left(e_{f,y_2} - e_{f,i/\theta}\right)$ for the capitalist farm. We have established all this in Chapter 3, through an appropriate characterisation of the values of the discount factors, λ_1 and λ_2. Now, if we note the terms on the R.H.S. and the L.H.S. of (4.15′) and recollect what we have known, again from our analysis in Chapter 3, about the relative significance of the elasticities of $\bar{P}C_1^I$ and A_2 with respect to their different arguments (e.g., the dominance of e_{ψ,y_1} over $(e_{\psi,w}$ or $e_{\psi,i}))$ and then judge the relative weights of the different terms on both sides of (4.15′), it becomes clear that given the values of $[\Delta y_1(t-1)/y_1(t-1)]$ (>0), $[\Delta y_2(t-1)/y_2(t-1)]$ (>0), g and other elasticities, if the difference between $\left(e_{\psi,y_1} - e_{\psi,i}\right)$ and $\left(e_{f,y_2} - e_{f,i/\theta}\right)$ is sufficiently high, then the condition (4.15′) will always come to hold. Therefore, in a dualistic economy where the distribution of income is known to be unequal and therefore the difference between $\left(e_{\psi,y_1} - e_{\psi,i}\right)$ and $\left(e_{f,y_2} - e_{f,i/\theta}\right)$ is known to be significant, the situation implied by (4.15′) is not a special situation, but a pointer towards a very general, and indeed, a real possibility.

Here, we can distinguish between two types of situations: (1) It may happen that in the case of a particular dualistic agriculture, the initial state itself is characterised by a value of y_1 which is so low both in absolute value and in relation to y_2 and therefore the difference between $\left(e_{\psi,y_1} - e_{\psi,i}\right)$ and $\left(e_{f,y_2} - e_{f,i/\theta}\right)$ is so great that (4.15′) comes to hold right in the beginning. This has the implication that this agriculture will never be able to come out of the initial stagnation. This is a case essentially similar to the one we have touched upon before.[2] (2) Alternatively, and perhaps more typically, the value of y_1, to start with, may not be that low and the value of y_2 that high so that (4.15′) may not hold in the beginning, and therefore there may be some capital accumulation going on. But, then, referring back to (4.10) it is clear that although $n\Delta K_1(t) + \Delta K_2(t)$ may be positive to start with, its algebraic value is related inversely with the difference $\left[\left(e_{\psi,y_1} - e_{\psi,i}\right) - \left(e_{f,y_1} - e_{f,i/\theta}\right)\right]$ falls and that of y_2 increases monotonically, $\left(e_{\psi,y_1} - e_{\psi,i}\right)$ keeps on increasing relative to $\left(e_{f,y_2} - e_{f,i/\theta}\right)$, and as a result the rate of capital accumulation starts falling, and there is again a definite tendency for the system to approach a state described by (4.15′).

We thus find that in a dualistic agriculture with an unequal distribution of income, there may exist, under very plausible conditions, an inherent tendency, either in the beginning or eventually, for capital accumulation to slow down, stop, or even become negative in the net sense. Given this tendency, the question which then naturally arises is: what are the ultimate limits of this capital path and, associated with it, the path of average income of the family farm?

Consider, first, the limit of the path of capital. If the production function in agriculture can be supposed to be such that a certain minimum amount of every factor, and in particular of capital, is essential for producing positive output; that is,

$$F\left(\overline{T}_i, K_i, L_i\right) = 0 \text{ for } K_i < K^*$$
$$> 0 \text{ for } K_i \geq K^*$$

where K^* is the essential requirement of capital and it is assumed that the essential quantities of other factors are available, then, given the general tendency of capital accumulation as mentioned before, the limit of the capital path is to end up with this minimum amount, and nothing more.

---

[2] See discussion of the case where the elasticity of M with respect to i is less than 1, pp. 41–43.

For the limit of $y_1(t)$, given that $\Delta y_1(t-1) \leq 0$ for all t (by Proposition 4), there are two possibilities:

1. $\lim_{t \to \infty} y_1(t) = A$, where A (> 0) is some constant. In this case, with the asymptote of $y_1(t)$ defined by a non-negative constant, although the net income of the family farm falls monotonically over time, there is no defaulting of loans. The relationship between the processes of income generation for the two types of farms, therefore, remains unchanged, and so also is the qualitative behaviour of the system over time. Only the family farm gets increasingly immiserised, and the inequality between the incomes of the capitalist and the family farm widens.
2. If, on the other hand, $y_1(t) = 0$ for some finite t, say, t^*, then there is a problem, because at the next period of time, as the capitalist farm, in trying to fulfil its objective (3.18), wants to ensure $\Delta y_1(t^*) \geq 0$ (Proposition 1), $y_1(t^* + 1)$ becomes negative. Given that

$$y(t) = \frac{\bar{P}F\left(\bar{T}_1, K_1(t), L_1(t)\right) + \left(w(t) - \mu\right)L_2(t)}{\bar{L}_1(t)} - \frac{i\bar{P}_k K_1(t) + \left(1 + i(t)\right)\bar{P}C_1^l(t)}{\bar{L}_1(t)},$$

this implies that the loan cannot be totally repaid from the family farm's gross income coming from wages and the value of output. Something has to give, and the way system accommodates this situation is through the mechanism of "distress sale" of land by the family farm to the capitalist farm. Such a transfer of land is supposed to take place in the event of any failure on the part of the family farm to repay its loan. However, since in the next period the capitalist farm will again want to ensure $\Delta y_2(t^* + 1) \geq 0$, the "distress sale of land" continues.[3] And, as it continues, a time may eventually come when all the land originally owned by the family farm will be taken over by the capitalist farm, and the family farmer will be reduced

---

[3] It should be noted that as a result of any increase in T_2 and fall in T_1, there is an increase in the marginal product of labour in the capitalist farm and a fall of it in the family farm, implying a reallocation of L_1 and L_2. Similarly, there is also an increase in the marginal product of capital in the capitalist farm and a fall of it in the family farm, again implying a reallocation of K_1 and K_2. But although there is change in the *composition* of the demand, the behaviour of the total *amount* of the demand for capital, $n\bar{P}_k K_1 + \bar{P}_k K_2$ relative to the demand for $\bar{P}C_1^l$ does not change, following the usual decrease in $y1$.

to the position of landless labour with wages earned from working in the capitalist farm as its only source of income.

But the process need not stop here if this wage is found to be above the subsistence level. Writing down the expressions of $\Delta y_1(t-1)$ and $\Delta y_2(t-1)$ which are just the discrete counterparts of (3.38) and (3.39),

$$\Delta y_1(t-1) = \frac{1}{\bar{L}_1(t-1)} \Big[\bar{P} F_{k1} \Delta K_1(t-1) + \big(w(t-1) - \mu\big) - g\bar{L}_1(t-1) \qquad (3.38')$$
$$+ \Delta w(t-1) L_2(t-1) - \Delta\{i(t-1) P_k K_1(t-1)$$
$$+ \big(1 + i(t-1)\big) \bar{P} C_1^l(t-1)\} - g Y_1(t-1) \Big]$$

$$\Delta y_2(t-1) = \frac{1}{\bar{L}_2(t-1)} \Big[\bar{P} F_{k2} \Delta K_2(t-1) - \Delta w(t-1) n L_2(t-1) \qquad (3.39')$$
$$+ \Delta\{i(t-1) M(t-1)\} - g Y_2(t-1) \Big]$$

and knowing that when the family farm is dispossessed of its land, $K_1(t-1) = 0$, $K_1(t-1) = 0$, $M(t-1) = n\bar{P}C_1^l(t-1)$, and $\bar{L}_1(t) = L_2(t)$, and that also, with (4.15') holding, $\Delta y_2(t-1) \leq 0$, we can see that the capitalist farm in trying to ensure, as a part of its objective, $\Delta y_2(t-1) \geq 0$, will still find it possible to increase the value of $\Delta\{i(t-1) M(t-1)\}$ and then ensure its repayment by deducting the corresponding amount from the payment of wage at the end of the period. The process finally stops when the wage rate in this way is reduced to the subsistence level.

We are therefore led to the following conclusion. If the agricultural sector of a less developed country is found to have the characteristics mentioned in Chapter 2, most importantly, if it is characterised by an unequal distribution of income between the family and capitalist farms, with the capitalist farms combining the operations of production and lending at the same time, and lending at the same time, and enjoying a monopolistic position in the latter, then, in the absence of any other exogenous factor, it is possible for the system to have an inherent tendency to remain in or approach a state of stagnation in capital accumulation. And, this is also likely to be accompanied by a process of immiserisation of the family farms with the possibility of an eventual polarisation between the capitalist farmers on the one hand and the family farmers, dispossessed of their land and reduced to the level of landless labourers at the subsistence level, on the other. Whether these inherent tendencies will in fact be realised in a particular situation will, of course, depend on the relative significance of other exogenous factors present in that situation and also on how closely the characteristics of the situation conform to the ones assumed in our analysis. We shall return to this question later on, in Chapter 6, when we shall consider the existence of such exogenous factors in terms of various types of technical progress and also the possibility of some variation in institutional characteristics, and see to what extent they may or may not prevent these tendencies from being realised in some real-life situations.

But, before that, we like to point out in a more precise form the significance of the distribution of income and the structure of credit market in generating these tendencies in a dualistic agriculture. The arguments to this effect have already been given in general terms, but, because of their importance to the central hypothesis of this presentation, we like to put these arguments in a more precise manner.

References

Bagchi, A. K. (2015). *Perilous Passage*. Lanham, MD: Rowman & Littlefield.
Bhaduri, A. (1983). *The Economic Structure of Backward Agriculture*. London: Academic Press.

CHAPTER 5

Significance of the Distribution of Income and Structure of Credit Market

Abstract The importance of distribution of income and structure of credit market as factors responsible for this crisis is brought out more precisely in this chapter, where the results of this model are compared with those of a hypothetical situation involving a more equal distribution of income and a more perfect credit market. It is shown that the two crucial issues—equalisation of income and perfection of the rural credit market—are essentially interconnected. It is therefore not possible to lessen this imperfection without improving the equality-content of distribution of income.

Keywords Inequality • Imperfection of credit market

To understand the importance of unequal distribution of income and imperfection of credit market as the factors responsible for these tendencies towards stagnation in capital accumulation and immiserisation of the family farms in a dualistic agriculture, it is important to single out the implications of these two factors from those of other forces in the system. We therefore propose to carry out a comparative analysis where the situation so long assumed in our model will be compared, from the standpoint of the question of capital accumulation, with another situation which will have all other characteristics, particularly, the per capita income of the entire agricultural sector and the rate of growth of population the same as

© The Author(s) 2018
A. K. Dasgupta, *Income Distribution, Market Imperfections and Capital Accumulation in a Developing Economy*,
https://doi.org/10.1007/978-981-13-1633-3_5

before, with the only exception that it will have a more equal distribution of income and a more perfect credit market.

It should be pointed out here that we consider these two crucial variations—more equalisation of incomes and more perfection of the credit market—as essentially interconnected. This is because we have seen in Chapter 2 that the factor crucially responsible for the imperfection of the credit market is the initial distribution of income whereby there are numerous family farms with a very low level of average income and therefore in need of credit, and a relatively few capitalist farms with a significantly higher level of average income and in a position to supply that credit. It is not possible to remove this imperfection without at the same time improving the distribution of income.[1] The two issues of equalisation of incomes and perfection of credit market are therefore to be considered together and their implications be studied jointly.

Consider, first, the existing situation in a dualistic agriculture with unequal distribution of income and imperfect credit market. Let $\bar{y}(t-1)$ be the net per capita income of this agriculture sector in the beginning of period t:

$$\bar{y}(t-1) = l_1(t-1)y_1(t-1) + l_2(t-1)y_2(t-1), \tag{5.1}$$

where $l_1(t-1)$ and $l_2(t-1)$ are the proportions of the family and capitalist farms in the total rural population. Let $\bar{x}(t-1) = y_1(t-1)/y_2(t-1)$ be the

---

[1] We have noted in this connection that there are certain administrative problems connected with credit operation in the rural areas which help preserve the monopoly power of the local capitalist farm as the money lender. But, we have also seen that these administrative problems are again fundamentally due to the family farms having a low level of income and small amount of asset (land). Hence any attempt to perfect the rural credit market by focusing attention only on the administrative problems and without any regard to the fundamental cause of these problems is likely to be self-defeating. In India, for example, the attempts to solve the problem by setting up the cooperative banks, unaccompanied by any change in the basic income and asset position of the family farms, have often ended up diverting funds in favour of the capitalist farms. To solve the problem, therefore, it is essential to think in terms of improving the average income (and asset holding) of the family farm. But improving the average income of the family farm will also imply, in a situation of not sufficiently high rate of capital accumulation and in the absence of any significant exogenous change, a reduction in the average income of the capitalist farm (by Preposition 3) and therefore a redistribution of income, at least in the beginning of the process.

index of inequality in the distribution of income and g, as before, the rate of growth of population in both the family and capitalist farms.

Consider, next, a new situation where the values of $\bar{y}_1(t-1)$ and g are the same as before, but where instead of letting $\bar{y}_1(t-1)$ and $\bar{y}_2(t-1)$ change according to the previous manner, a policy intervention is made through, say, a measure of land reform or an agricultural income tax-cum-subsidy, which has the effect of redistributing a definite amount of income from the capitalist to the family farm over the period t. This is a case of pure income redistribution without any overall change in $\bar{y}(t-1)$ so that

$$\Delta y_1(t-1) = -\frac{l_2(t-1)}{l_1(t-1)} \Delta y_2(t-1) > 0 \tag{5.2}$$

In this new situation, following the increase in $y_1(t-1)$ there will be a reduction, for reasons already mentioned, in the value of $\theta(t)$ implying a lessening of imperfection in the credit market. In fact, if the equalisation of income is sufficiently complete, the value of $\theta(t)$ will tend to fall to 1 which is the state of perfect credit market.

The question, now, is what is the effect of this move from the original to the new situation, of this redistribution of income and perfection of credit market, on the rate of capital accumulation? It should be noted that so far the changes in the parameters in the new situation are concerned, the changes in $\bar{L}_1(t)$ and $\bar{L}_2(t)$ are the same as before, but the changes in $y_1(t-1)$ and $y_2(t-1)$ are now exactly in the opposite direction, with $\Delta y_1(t-1)/y_1(t-1) > 0$ and $\Delta y_2(t-1)/y_2(t-1) > 0$. To analyse the effect of these new qualitative change in $y_1(t-1)$ and $y_2(t-1)$, as brought about by the redistribution of income, on the rate of aggregate capital accumulation we have to refer to the crucial condition (4.15)'.

On observing the terms in (4.15)', it becomes clear that following these changes in $y_1(t-1)$ and $y_2(t-1)$ and a consequent fall in $\theta(t)$ there will be changes in both sides of (4.15)' as compared to the original situation. On the R.H.S., as a result of an increase in $y_1(t-1)$, there will be, on the one hand, a fall in $\bar{P}C_1^l(t)$ and hence a change in the fourth term; on the other hand, due to a consequent fall in $\theta(t)$ and $i(t)$, there will be an increase in $\bar{P}C_1^l(t)$ and therefore a change in the second term. Summing up these two changes, we get the total change in $\bar{P}C_1^l(t)$: $n\bar{P}C_1^l(t)\left[e_{\psi,i}\,e_{i},\theta^e\theta,y_1\Delta y_1(t-1)/y_1(t-1) - e_{\psi,y_i}\,\Delta y_1(t-1)/y_1(t-1)\right]$ as a result of moving to the new situation.

Similarly, on the L.H.S. there will be two kinds of changes as compared to the original situation. Since there is a fall in $y_2(t-1)$, this, by itself, will mean a fall in $A_2(t)$ (a change in the third term). At the same time, because of a fall in $y_1(t-1)$ and a fall in $\theta(t)$, and therefore a rise in $i(t)/\theta(t)$, there will also be a positive effect on $A_2(t)$ (a change in the first term). Adding these two changes, we get

$$A_2(t)\left[e_{f,i}/\theta^e i/\theta,\theta^e\theta,y_1 \Delta y_1(t-1)/y_1(t-1) + e_{f,y_2}\Delta y_2(t-1)/y_2(t-1)\right].$$

Now, if the resulting total change in the L.H.S. exceeds the corresponding total change in the R.H.S., that is, if

$$A_2(t)\left[e_{f,i}/\theta^e i/\theta,\theta^e\theta,y_1 \Delta y_1(t-1)/y_1(t-1) + e_{f,y_2}\Delta y_2(t-1)/y_2(t-1)\right] \quad (5.3)$$
$$> n\bar{P}C_1^l(t)\left[e_{\psi,i}e_i,\theta^e\theta,y_1 \Delta y_1(t-1)/y_1(t-1) + e_{\psi,y_1}\Delta y_1(t-1)/y_1(t-1)\right]$$
$$-e_{\psi,y_1}\Delta y_1(t-1)/y_1(t-1)$$

that is, by using (5.2) so that $\Delta y_2(t-1) = -\dfrac{l_1(t-1)}{l_2(t-1)}\Delta y_1(t-1)$ and also the definition of $\bar{x}(t-1)$, if

$$A_2(t)\left[e_{f,i}/\theta^e i/\theta,\theta^e\theta,y_1 - e_{f,y_2}x(t-1)\frac{l_1(t-1)}{l_2(t-1)}\right] \quad (5.4)$$
$$> n\bar{P}C_1^l(t)\left[e_{\psi,i}e_i,\theta^e\theta,_{y_1} - e_{\psi,y_1}\right],$$

then we can conclude that, as a result of the redistribution of income and consequent lessening of imperfection in the credit market, $A_2(t)$ in the new situation will tend to increase faster than $\bar{P}C_1^l(t)$ in algebraic value, implying therefore that there will be a definite increase in the rate of capital accumulation.

Now, we already know from our analysis in Chapter 3 that when the distribution of income between the family and capitalist farms is such that the family farm has a level of average income which is very low both in absolute amount and in relation to the capitalist farm, then the difference between the income and the interest elasticity of the demand of the family farm for consumption loan is always significantly greater than the corresponding holding of wealth by the capitalist farm. Therefore, in the context of the present comparison when the distribution of income is known to be unequal to start with, that is, given the value of $l_1(t-1)/l_2(t-1)$, $x(t-1)$ is known to be sufficiently low, the difference $\left(e_{\psi,y_1} - e_{\psi,i}\right)$ is expected to be significantly greater than the difference $\left(e_{f,y_2} - e_{f,i/\theta}\right)$ and therefore, given the ratio between $A_2(t)$ and $\bar{P}C_1^l$ and other elasticities, it is clear that in such a situation (5.4) is very likely to hold. In other words, if the distribution of income is significantly unequal and the credit market imperfect, it is quite possible to promote capital accumulation by redistributing that income and lessening the imperfection in the credit market.

It is of some importance to compare this conclusion with a well-known traditional wisdom which has always tended to uphold inequality as an argument for promoting capital accumulation. For the purpose of this comparison it is useful to rewrite (5.4) as

$$\left[\frac{\partial A_2}{\partial i/\theta}\frac{\partial i/\theta}{\partial \theta}\frac{\partial \theta}{\partial y_1} - n\frac{\partial \bar{P}C_1^l}{\partial i}\frac{\partial i}{\partial \theta}\frac{\partial \theta}{\partial y_1}\right] > \left[\frac{\partial A_2}{\partial y_2}\frac{l_1(t-1)}{l_2(t-1)} + n\frac{\partial \bar{P}C_1^l}{\partial y_1}\right] \quad (5.4')$$

which is obtained by substituting the definitions of the elasticities and transferring the terms between the two sides. By the mean value theorem once again, the derivatives in this expression are to be considered as evaluated at some appropriate interior points of the respective intervals.

The crux of the traditional argument is that the marginal propensity to save of the poorer income group can be taken to be lower than that of the richer group, and therefore any equalisation of incomes will lower the amount of aggregate saving and reduce the rate of capital accumulation. Now, translating this argument in terms of our analytical framework, where the wealth holding of the capitalist farm is to be taken as the equivalent of the saving of the rich and the consumption loan of the family farm, that is, the (negative) saving of the poor, we find that the basic contention of this traditional hypothesis has the effect of rendering the R.H.S. of (5.4′) positive and, by implication, since the interaction between income and interest has not been considered in this hypothesis, the L.H.S. zero. With the R.H.S. thus exceeding the L.H.S., it is clear from (5.4′), or its equivalent formulation (5.4), that one can then get a conclusion by which any equalisation of income will appear as detrimental to capital accumulation.

There is, however, a crucial assumption relating to the effect of the process of income redistribution that underlies the core of this traditional argument. The assumption, it seems, is that the redistribution of income is a neutral phenomenon so far its effects on the institutional structure of the economy are concerned; apart from immediately affecting the income terms in the saving function, it does not affect the structure of the economy at all; it does not, for example, affect the structure of any market.

This assumption of neutrality, however, need not always be true, and it is particularly not true for a dualistic agriculture of a less developed country. In such agriculture we have seen that the structure of the credit market is crucially connected with the existing state of the distribution of income between the family and capitalist farms, with the result that a redistribution of income in favour of the former always has the effect of lessening the imperfection of this structure. Under this situation, therefore, any equalisation of incomes, in addition to having an "income effect" which may tend to reduce the supply of aggregate wealth (the R.H.S. of (5.4')) and which alone was considered in the traditional argument, will also have, through the perfection of credit market, an important "interest effect" which will be seen in terms of a fall in the rate of interest and a rise in the marginal rate of return on wealth (the L.H.S. of (5.4')), and which will tend to increase the availability of wealth for capital accumulation. And, if this interest effect of income redistribution dominates its income effect, and we have explained that there are plausible conditions under which it very well may, then the final effect on capital accumulation will be very different from what was suggested in the traditional argument.

Finally, there is an important dynamic implication of this perfection of credit market. We have seen that although both the family and capitalist farms want to ensure, as a part of their objective, that $\Delta y_i(t-1) \geq 0 \, (i=1,2)$, under imperfect credit market, it is only the capitalist farm which succeeds in achieving it because then it has a prior advantage of choosing the amount of saving through which it can affect the value of the rate of interest. However, once the imperfection of credit market is removed, the capitalist farm will no longer have any advantage to ensure $\Delta y_2(t-1) \geq 0$. As a result, it can now be equally possible for $\Delta y_1(t-1) \geq 0$, and should that happen, it will also become possible, because of the nature of the elasticities of $\bar{P}C_1^f(t)$ and $A_2(t)$, for capital accumulation to keep on increasing. Thus, the effect of equalisation of incomes and perfection of credit market initiated in any particular period need not be restricted to that period only; it can indeed open up the possibility of increase in capital accumulation on a permanent basis.

When capital accumulation keeps taking place in this way, a time may eventually come when it will be possible for the system to cross that threshold value of capital accumulation subject to which Proposition 3 was found valid. And if Proposition 3 is rendered ineffective, it will then be possible for both y_1 and y_2 to increase over time and we will have a situation where not only the blocks on capital accumulation will be removed, but the tendency towards the immiserisation of the family farm will also be reversed.

Thus in a dualistic agriculture comparing the existing situation of unequal distribution of income and imperfection of the credit market with a situation of more equalised incomes and perfected credit market, and observing how the possibilities of significant increase in capital accumulation can be opened up by moving towards the latter situation, one can come to understand the crucial importance of the existing state of income distribution and the structure of credit market as the factors responsible for aborting these possibilities and perpetuating instead a tendency towards stagnation.

* * *

The central idea of this presentation, that the insufficiency of capital accumulation in a dualistic agriculture can be explained in terms of the existing distribution of income and the imperfection of credit market, needs to be carefully distinguished from some other hypotheses in the literature. It has to be distinguished, for example, from the usual "vicious circles of poverty" hypothesis which, in essence, suggests that an underdeveloped country tends to remain underdeveloped because, given its small per capita income, it can hardly generate any significant amount of saving at the aggregate level. And, ruling out the possibility of any large-scale inflow of foreign capital except in some special situations, this limitation on the aggregate saving also implies a corresponding limitation on the accumulation of capital, and hence the economy is trapped in a kind of low-level equilibrium. The problem is further compounded, it is added, by the fact that most of these underdeveloped countries are also in their second phase of demographic evolution, experiencing a high rate of population growth.

What we have shown, on the other hand, it that it is possible to offer an alternative explanation of the phenomenon of underdevelopment by shifting the focus of analysis, which in these traditional hypotheses has only been on the central tendency of the distribution of income, to the dispersion of the distribution and the structure of credit market that results from this dispersion. We have shown that given the existing per capita income and the rate of growth of population as they are in a less developed country, it may be possible, just by redistributing income more equally and breaking down imperfection of the credit market, to generate enough saving from which capital accumulation can be initiated. One can then further argue that if this capital accumulation and therefore the growth of income are sustained long enough, that by itself may lead to a demographic reversal.

Our argument needs also to be contrasted with a sociological hypothesis according to which the failure of a less developed country to generate capital accumulation is to be explained in terms of the lack of appropriate sociocultural factors. We think, however, that one may not necessarily have to go for this kind of exogenisation of explanation. It is possible, as we have shown in the context of a dualistic agriculture, to explain this phenomenon of stagnation in basic economic terms, in terms of the decisions taken by the family and capitalist farms to satisfy their economic objective under the special circumstances produced by the unequal distribution of income and the imperfection of credit market. It is shown that with the distribution of income and the structure of credit market as they are, the capitalist farmer will always find it worthwhile to restrict the amount of saving as well as its allocation to productive use to a certain level, determined, among others, by the interest elasticity of the market demand for loan, not necessarily because of any cultural inhibition but because given his economic objective, that is the most profitable thing to do.

References

Bhaduri, A. (1983). *The Economic Structure of Backward Agriculture.* London: Academic Press.
Stiglitz, J. E. (2015). *The Great Divide.* New York: W.W. Norton & Company.

CHAPTER 6

Different Ways of Resolving the Crisis

Abstract Several ways of resolving this problem of inadequate capital accumulation in a developing economy are discussed, including especially the solution that is offered by technical progress as well as land reforms. But here again, it is found that even this technical progress–based solution also depends on the nature of initial distribution of income.

Keywords Land reforms • Technical progress

Given the tendency of a dualistic agriculture to approach a state of stagnation in capital accumulation, the question which naturally arises is this: Are there ways in which this tendency can be reversed and the system lifted out of this impasse? The following possibilities are suggested.

1. Suppose that the agricultural sector has reached the state of stagnation where (4.15′) holds and where all land of the family farms has been taken over by the capitalist farm and the wage rate has been reduced to the subsistence level. When the system is actually pushed to this extreme situation, interestingly enough, it also acquires a potentially redeeming feature. This is because, with all land of the family farms taken over and the wage at the subsistence level, it is no longer possible for the capitalist farm to ensure $\Delta y_2(t-1) \geq 0$ (which, as we know from Proposition 1, is necessary to fulfil its basic objective (3.18)), by either increasing the interest earnings or reducing the wage payment. In other words, with these two channels closed, there

© The Author(s) 2018
A. K. Dasgupta, *Income Distribution, Market Imperfections and Capital Accumulation in a Developing Economy*,
https://doi.org/10.1007/978-981-13-1633-3_6

is no way for the capitalist farm to increase, or hold constant, its per capita net income at the expense of the other group. To ensure $\Delta y_2(t-1) \geq 0$ in this situation, it is clear from (3.39′) (since the second and third terms on the R.H.S. are reduced to zero) that the capitalist farm will now have to start accumulating capital. As a result, we can have two possibilities:

(a) This rate of accumulation of capital in the very first iteration may be so high and therefore, given the complementarity with labour, the increase in the wage rate and through that the increase in $y_1(t-1)$ so significant that, with the elasticities of $\bar{P}C_1^I(t)$ and $A_2(t)$ with respect to different arguments as they are, there may be a reversal in the direction of inequality in (4.15′). If this happens, then, of course, a breakthrough will be initiated, and the stagnation will turn out to be self-correcting.

(b) More typically, however, the rate of capital accumulation in the very first instance may not be that high and the increase in the wage rate and $y_1(t-1)$ not that significant so that (4.5′) may continue to hold. This implies that, with the initial capital accumulation, as the wage rate is only increased from its previous subsistence level, the capitalist farm at the next iteration will find it again most profitable to be able to ensure $\Delta y_2(t) \geq 0$ by increasing the value of interest earning, and then getting it repaid by subtracting the corresponding amount from the wage payment, until the wage rate again falls back to the subsistence level. In other words, stagnation of dualistic agriculture can be stable in the small and unstable only in the large. It is interesting that we come to this well-known result in the development literature,[1] *but for very different reasons.*

If, therefore, there are reasons to believe that from a state of stagnation the system may not always self-initiate capital accumulation at a rate high enough to disturb the local stability, then one has to think in terms of some change in the institutional structure or in terms of exogenous factors to dislodge the system from its low-level equilibrium and bring about global instability in the right direction.

2. We shall first take up the question of institutional change, and here we shall start by considering the possibility of such a change in the structure of the labour market. Suppose that we think of a different situation in the labour market where, unlike what has been assumed so far, the family farmers or, in the extreme case, the landless labourers organise themselves in each set and act as a group rather than as atomistic individuals in supplying labour to the capitalist farm. The implication of this institutional change is

---

[1] Leibenstin, H. *Economic Backwardness* (1957), Chs. 1–4.

that corresponding to the monopolistic situation on the supply side of the credit market, there is now monopoly also on the supply side of the labour market. In our analysis, so far, only the capitalist farm had the power to ensure $\Delta y_2(t-1) \geq 0$ because, given its monopolistic control in the credit market, it had the one-sided advantage of controlling the amount of savings and, through that, increasing their interest earnings. But, now, with a corresponding monopoly power in the labour market, the family farms, or landless labourers, as the case may be, have a similar advantage in their choice of the amount of labour to be supplied by which they can control the wage earnings and thus also ensure $\Delta y_1(t-1) \geq 0$ (cf. the eq. (3.38′)). Therefore, depending on the balance of monopoly power in the two markets, it is now quite possible to have a situation where $\Delta y_1(t-1) \geq 0$. And, once that happens, we have seen in Chapter 5 that it also becomes possible, given the elasticities of $\bar{P}C_1^l(t)$ and $A_1(t)$ with respect to the relevant arguments, for capital accumulation to be initiated on a permanent basis. This is an interesting example of how the stagnation in agriculture can be resolved through an institutional change in the labour market. However, since this solution implies that at least in the initial stage of capital accumulation $\Delta y_2(t-1) < 0$, in suggesting this solution one should also be aware of the type of resistance that is to come from the capitalist farms against the implementation of this kind of change.

3. Another kind of institutional change which is more usually considered, and we also have mentioned it is Chapter 5, is a policy of land reforms which can change the ownership of land in favour of the family farms. To the extent that such a policy can be implemented in a significant scale, it has the same qualitative effect on y_1 as is obtained from a change in the structure of labour market mentioned above, and, therefore, it has the same kind of potential for breaking the stagnation in capital accumulation. The development-enhancing effect of land reforms has also been comprehensively studied from farm-level data for about 700 farms in West Bengal (where some significant land reforms were carried out in 1982–1995) when it is found that the general equilibrium effects of land reforms may actually be much stronger than the partial equilibrium effects (Bardhan, Mukherjee and Kumar, Journal of Development Economics, 2011).

4. From these considerations of internal institutional changes let us now pass on to the question of the so-called exogenous changes in the system and see how the crisis in capital accumulation can be resolved through them. Of all the vehicles of such changes, the one which is most commonly considered is technical progress. Conceived exogenously, this technical progress can be represented as a function of time:

$$\lambda = \lambda(t), \tag{6.1}$$

where λ is the indicator of technical progress. Here, for the convenience of working with differential operator, we are again working in terms of continuous time. Reinterpretation of the results in terms of period analysis should be immediate.

Assuming that the incidence of this technical progress is the same on both the family and capitalist farms, λ can be introduced as another factor in the production function of both the farms,[2] and (3.2′) and (3.14) be rewritten as

$$y_1 = \frac{\overline{P}F(\overline{T}_1, K_1, L_1; \lambda) + (w - \mu)L_2}{\overline{L}_1} - \frac{i\overline{P}_k K_1 + (1+i)\overline{P}C_1^I}{\overline{L}_1}, \tag{6.2}$$

and

$$y_2 = \frac{\overline{P}F(\overline{T}_2, K_2, nL_2; \lambda) - wnL_2}{\overline{L}_2} + \frac{iM + n\overline{P}C_1^I}{\overline{L}_2} \tag{6.3}$$

where w and i will now depend also on λ; that is,

$$w = \overline{P}F_{L1}(\overline{T}_1, K_1, L_1; \lambda) + \mu = \overline{P}F_{L2}(\overline{T}_2, K_2, nL_2; \lambda), \tag{6.4}$$

and

$$i = \frac{\overline{P}}{\overline{P}_k}(F_{k1}\overline{T}_1, K_1, L_1; \lambda) = \theta \frac{\overline{P}}{\overline{P}_k} F_{k2}(\overline{T}_2, K_2, nL_2; \lambda) \tag{6.5}$$

Clearly then,

$$\left.\frac{dw}{dt}\right|_\lambda = \frac{dw}{dt} + \overline{P}\frac{\partial F_{L1}}{\partial \lambda}\frac{d\lambda}{dt} = \frac{dw}{dt} + \overline{P}\frac{\partial F_{L2}}{\partial \lambda}\frac{d\lambda}{dt} \tag{6.6}$$

---

[2] Note that we are representing technical progress in its most general form, avoiding, for example, its representation in terms of the factor-augmenting form which is essentially a restrictive case. See Burmeister, E. and Dobell, A., *Mathematical Theories of Economic Growth*, pp. 67–77.

where $dw/dt|_\lambda$ is the total change in the wage rate with respect to time taking into account the effect of technical progress and dw/dt is the change in the same in the absence of technical progress, that is, the kind of change we had so long been considering.

Similarly,

$$\left.\frac{di}{dt}\right|_\lambda = \frac{di}{dt} + \frac{\bar{P}}{\bar{P}_k}\frac{\partial F_{k1}}{\partial \lambda}\frac{d\lambda}{dt} = \frac{di}{dt} + \theta\frac{\bar{P}}{\bar{P}_k}\frac{\partial F_{k2}}{\partial \lambda}\frac{d\lambda}{dt}. \quad (6.7)$$

Furthermore, using the property of homogeneity of degree one of F in T_i, K_i and L_i and, therefore, homogeneity of degree zero in the partial derivatives of F, and also the property of continuity of the second-order partial derivatives of F, we have[3]

$$\frac{\partial F}{\partial \lambda}(\bar{T}_1, K_1, L_1; \lambda) = \bar{T}_1 \frac{\partial F_{T1}}{\partial \lambda}\frac{d\lambda}{dt} + K_1\frac{\partial F_{k1}}{\partial \lambda}\frac{d\lambda}{dt} + L_1\frac{\partial F_{L1}}{\partial \lambda}\frac{d\lambda}{dt} \quad (6.8)$$

and

$$\frac{\partial F}{\partial \lambda}(\bar{T}_2, K_2, L_2, \lambda) = \bar{T}_2 \frac{\partial F_{T2}}{\partial \lambda}\frac{d\lambda}{dt} + K_2\frac{\partial F_{k2}}{\partial \lambda}\frac{d\lambda}{dt} + nL_2\frac{\partial F_{L2}}{\partial \lambda}\frac{d\lambda}{dt}, \quad (6.9)$$

---

[3] **Proof:** By the property of homogeneity of degree one of F with respect to Ti, Ki, and Li, we have, for example, in the case of the family farms $F(\bar{T}_1, K_1, L_1, \lambda) = \bar{T}_1 F_{T1}(\bar{T}_1, K_1, L_1; \lambda) + K_1 F_{k1}(\bar{T}_1, K_1, L_1; \lambda) + L_1 F_{L1} F(\bar{T}_1, K_1, L_i; \lambda)$.

Now, totally differentiating both sides with respect to t, we get, upon cancelling out the common terms and regrouping the terms,

$$\frac{\partial F}{\partial \lambda}\frac{d\lambda}{dt} = \frac{dk_1}{dt}\left[\bar{T}_1 \frac{\partial F_{T1}}{\partial K_1} + K_1\frac{\partial F_{k1}}{\partial K_1} + L_1\frac{\partial F_{L1}}{\partial K_1}\right] + \frac{dL_1}{dt}\left[\bar{T}_1 \frac{\partial F_{T1}}{\partial L_1} + K_1\frac{\partial F_{k1}}{\partial L_1} + L_1\frac{\partial F_{L1}}{\partial K_1}\right]$$
$$+ \left[\bar{T}_1 \frac{\partial F_{T1}}{\partial L_1} + K_1\frac{\partial F_{k1}}{\partial L_1} + L_1\frac{\partial F_{L1}}{\partial K_1}\right].$$

By the property of continuity of the second-order partial derivatives and homogeneity of degree zero of the partial derivatives, the first two terms of the R.H.S. are zero. Hence the required result.

so that, taking into account technical progress in this most general form, that is, allowing for the possibility of technical progress affecting the marginal product of every factor, the original expressions for dy_1/dt and dy_2/dt given by (3.22) and (3.23), can be rewritten as

$$\frac{dy_1}{dt} = \frac{1}{\bar{L}_1}\left[\bar{P}F_{k1}\frac{dK_1}{dt}+\bar{T}_1\bar{P}\frac{\partial F_{T1}}{\partial \lambda}\frac{d\lambda}{dt}+K_1\bar{P}\frac{\partial F_{k1}}{\partial \lambda}\frac{d\lambda}{dt}+L_1\bar{P}\frac{\partial F_{L1}}{\partial \lambda}\frac{d\lambda}{dt}+(w-\mu)g\bar{L}_1\right.$$

$$\left.+\left(\frac{dw}{dt}+\bar{P}\frac{\partial F_{L2}}{\partial \lambda}\frac{d\lambda}{dt}\right)L_2-\frac{d}{dt}\left(iP_kK_1+(1+i)PC_1^l\right)-\frac{\bar{P}}{\bar{P}},\frac{\partial F_{k1}}{\partial \lambda}\frac{d\lambda}{dt}PC_1^l-gY_1\right]$$

(6.10)

and

$$\frac{dy_2}{dt} = \frac{1}{\bar{L}_2}\left[\bar{P}F_{k2}\frac{dk_2}{dt}+\bar{T}_2\bar{P}\frac{\partial F_{T2}}{\partial \lambda}\frac{d\lambda}{dt}+K_2\bar{P}\frac{\partial F_{k2}}{\partial \lambda}\frac{d\lambda}{dt}+nL_2\bar{P}\frac{\partial F_{L2}}{\partial \lambda}\frac{d\lambda}{dt}\right.$$

$$\left.-\left(\frac{dw}{dt}+\bar{P}\frac{\partial F_{L2}}{\partial \lambda}\frac{d\lambda}{dt}\right)nL_2+\frac{d}{dt}(iM)+\frac{\bar{P}}{\bar{P}}\frac{\partial F_{K1}}{\partial \lambda}\frac{d\lambda}{dt}M-gY_2\right]$$

(6.11)

For the purpose of our analysis, we now make a distinction between (a) labour-using technical progress which will be defined by

$$n_iL_i\frac{\partial F_{Li}}{\partial \lambda}\frac{d\lambda}{dt} > K_i\frac{\partial F_{ki}}{\partial \lambda}\frac{d\lambda}{dt}+\bar{T}_1\frac{\partial F_{Ti}}{\partial \lambda}\frac{d\lambda}{dt},\qquad(6.12)$$

and (b) non-labour-using technical progress which will be defined as

$$n_iL_i\frac{\partial F_{Li}}{\partial \lambda}\frac{d\lambda}{dt} \leq K_i\frac{\partial F_{ki}}{\partial \lambda}\frac{d\lambda}{dt}+\bar{T}_1\frac{\partial F_{Ti}}{\partial \lambda}\frac{d\lambda}{dt},\qquad(6.13)$$

$i = 1, 2$, and $n_i = 1$ for $i = 1$.

(a) In the case of labour-using technical progress, if the increase in the productivity of labour is sufficiently significant, particularly, relative to the increase in the productivity of capital, so that

$$\bar{P}\left(\frac{\partial F_{L1}}{\partial \lambda}L_1 + \frac{\partial F_{L2}}{\partial \lambda}L_2\right)\frac{d\lambda}{dt} > \frac{\bar{P}}{\bar{P}_k}\frac{\partial F_{k1}}{\partial \lambda}\frac{d\lambda}{dt}\bar{P}C_1^l - \bar{T}_1\bar{P}\frac{\partial F_{T1}}{\partial \lambda}\frac{d\lambda}{dt} - \frac{dw}{dt}$$
$$-(w-\mu)g\bar{L}_1 + \frac{di}{dt}\left(\bar{P}_k K_1 + \bar{P}C_1^l\right) + (1+i)\frac{d\bar{P}C_1^l}{dt} + gY_1. \qquad (6.14)$$

Then, as evident from (6.10), it is possible for y_1 of the family farm to increase over time. And, so far the capitalist farm is concerned, *in the beginning* it is also possible for them to ensure the non-negativity of dy_2/dt as before, because no matter how significant the basis of technical progress in favour of labour is, any increase in w due to technical progress is compensated by an equivalent increase in the productivity of labour (see eq. 6.11). Now, with y_1 increasing and y_2 non-decreasing, there will be both a downward pull on $\bar{P}C_1^l$ and an upward pull on A_2 (since there will be an additional positive effect through the increase in i/θ), and it is clear from (5.3) that in such a situation there is bound to be an increase in capital accumulation. And, if this situation is maintained, the stagnation in agriculture can indeed be overcome.

However, there is a different problem which is likely to arise in this case from the standpoint of capitalist farm, and for the following reason. As capital keeps accumulating and y_1 increasing, a time may eventually come when it will be possible for the family farm to self-finance its consumption as well as production needs, thus getting rid of the imperfect credit market altogether. But, this will also mean a total loss of one source of income for the capitalist farm, as will be seen by the disappearance of the two terms, $d/dt(iM)$ and $\bar{P}/\bar{P}_k \partial F_{k1}/\partial \lambda\, d\lambda/dt\, M$, on the R.H.S. of (6.11). And, in a situation where $K_2\bar{P}\partial F_{k2}/\partial \lambda d\lambda/dt + \bar{T}_2\bar{P}\partial F_{T2}/\partial \lambda d\lambda/dt$ is not significant, this may indeed imply $dy_2/dt < 0$ eventually. Thus, the capitalist farms may have more to lose than gain from a labour-using technical progress. And, therefore, to the extent that they as a group have any control over the introduction of this technical progress, it is possible that they will effectively resist that introduction, although it is clear that this kind of technical progress, if introduced, can indeed solve the problem of agricultural stagnation.

In real life, technical progress of this kind is best illustrated by education, particularly by a productivity-oriented education in the rural areas. And it may be interesting to explain and interpret, in the light of the analysis just made, the kind of inadequate attention that is found to exist in the government policy regarding education in some of the less developed countries which have agricultural situation similar to the one being discussed here.[4]

(b) Turning now to non-labour-using technical progress, we find that even here it is possible for y_1 to keep increasing because, as is clear from (6.13), there can always be some increase in the marginal product of labour, and therefore there is again a danger of an eventual loss of credit market and interest earnings from the standpoint of the capitalist farm. However, it is now possible to distinguish between two types of situations depending on whether

$$K_2 \bar{P} \frac{\partial F_{k2}}{\partial \lambda} \frac{d\lambda}{dt} + \bar{T}_2 \bar{P} \frac{\partial F_{T2}}{\partial \lambda} \frac{d\lambda}{dt} < \left(\frac{dw}{dt} + \bar{P} \frac{F_{L2}}{\partial \lambda} \frac{d\lambda}{dt} \right) nL_2 - \bar{P} F_{k2} \frac{dK_2}{dt} + gY_2 \quad (6.15)$$

$$K_2 \bar{P} \frac{\partial F_{k2}}{\partial \lambda} \frac{d\lambda}{dt} + \bar{T}_2 \bar{P} \frac{\partial F_{T2}}{\partial \lambda} \frac{d\lambda}{dt} \geq \left(\frac{dw}{dt} + \bar{P} \frac{\partial F_{L2}}{\partial \lambda} \frac{d\lambda}{dt} \right) nL_2 - \bar{P} F_{k2} \frac{dK_2}{dt} + gY_2 \quad (6.16)$$

at a time t^* where the source of interest income may have been totally lost.

In the first case, it is possible for y_1 and, in the beginning, also for y_2 to increase and therefore, for reasons already mentioned, there will be again a good possibility of achieving a breakthrough in capital accumulation. But, once again, there may be resistance on the part of capitalist farm in this situation, because although it is a case of technical progress which is biased in favour of land and capital, it is still possible for y_1 to increase sufficiently to cause loss of interest earnings for the capitalist farm without the increases in the marginal products of capital and land being significant enough to compensate for that loss. It is only when the bias in technical progress for capital and land is sufficiently high to assure the capitalist farm an overcompensating gain through the increases in the marginal products of capital and land in the event of a possible loss of credit market that the capitalist farm will be found motivated to adopt the technical progress. This situation is shown by the second case (6.16).

---

[4] In the context of India, for example, one finds that the government policy has in fact been systematically biased against this required education throughout the period of planning. See Bhagwati, J.: "Education, Class Structure and Income Inequality," *World Development*, Vol. 1, May 1973, p. 24; for similar phenomenon in other less developed countries, see Bowles, S.: "Class Power and Mass Education," Harvard University, 1971.

There are two interesting implications that come out of this analysis. In the first place, it is clear that in a dualistic agriculture, where the capitalist farm, because of the existing distribution of income, is more likely to have the effective power in adopting any technical change, the existence of knowledge of a technical progress, by itself, is not enough for its implementation, no matter how powerful it may be to dislodge the agriculture from its stagnation. Technical progress has to be of a particular type, especially biased in favour of capital and land in order to be adopted in the system. The type of technical progress which in real life comes close to this description is the so-called Green Revolution, which is supposed to increase productivity of every factor, but proportionately more of land and capital.

Second, even with the knowledge of a non-labour-using technical progress like the Green Revolution, its acceptance will be easier when the opportunity cost of adopting such a change is not significant for the capitalist farm, where the opportunity cost is measured by the interest earnings to be forgone in the event of a loss of the credit market. This opportunity cost, in its turn, depends on the degree of jointness with which the two operations—capitalist farming and money lending—are performed by a single group. Therefore, the less identified these activities are with one economic group, the less is the opportunity cost and higher is the prospect for adoption of my given kind of non-labour-using technical progress.

It is of some importance to mention this last point, because it may help to explain the differential impact that the Green Revolution is found to have on different parts of the dualistic agriculture of a country like India. Apart from the fact that the knowledge of this technical progress is itself more developed in certain crop pattern than others (which in terms of our model means that different values of $(\partial F_{Ti}/\partial \lambda \; d\lambda/dt + \partial F_{Ki}/\partial \lambda \; d\lambda/dt)$ are available for different regions specialising in particular crops), it should also be carefully noted that the success of the Green Revolution has been found to be weaker in those parts of India where the operations of money lending and capitalist farming are closely identified with one single group, and found to be stronger in those parts where, for some interesting historical and institutional reasons, this identification is far less complete.[5]

---

[5] See Bhaduri, Amit, 'A Study in Agricultural Backwardness under Semi-Feudalism', *Economic Journal*, March 1973, pp. 120–122.

We conclude, therefore, by observing that there do exist quite a few potential solutions to the problem of agricultural stagnation in a less developed country. However, it is also found that unless the institutional structure happens to be particularly propitious (with an appropriate separation between the money lending and the farming activities) or technical progress of an especially biased nature (a) sufficiently high value of ($\partial F_{Ti}/\partial \lambda \, d\lambda/dt + \partial F_{Ki}/\partial \lambda \, d\lambda/dt$) many of these solutions [such as the possibilities (2), (3) and (4)] call for a change which is likely to go against the interest of the capitalist farmers. And, in the context of a society where certain political power may exist in the hands of these farmers, this analysis draws our attention to a kind of constraints on economic development, very different from the ones suggested in the conventional analysis.

References

Bhagawati, J. (1973). Education, Class Structure and Income Inequality. *World Development, 1*, 24.

Bowles, S. (1977). *Class Power and Mass Education*. Cambridge, MA: Harvard University.

Burmeister, E., & Dobell, A. (1933). *Mathematical Theories of Economic Growth* (pp. 67–77). Aldershot: Gregg Revivals.

CHAPTER 7

Some Other Results in the Literature

Abstract In this chapter, conclusions of the model presented here are compared with other results in the literature, particularly where the issues of income distribution have been considered.

Keywords Imperfections of labour market and credit market
• Dualistic Agriculture

Although much has been written about the dualism between the agricultural and industrial sectors of an underdeveloped economy, the literature on the dualism that exists within the agricultural sector is not very extensive. The existence of a dualistic agriculture was mentioned by Sen,[1] and an analysis of the problem of resource allocation within this structure came to be developed also in the writings of Eckaus. On the questions of income distribution and capital accumulation in such agriculture, the issues which are of more immediate concern to us, the two important works are by Bardhan[2] and Bhaduri.[3]

---

[1] Sen, Amartya K., "Peasants and Dualism with or without Surplus Labour," Journal of Political Economy, Vol. 74, October 1966.

[2] Bardhan, Pranab K., "A Model of Growth of Capitalism in a Dual Agrarian Economy" in Bhagwati & Eckaus (eds): Essays in Honour of Rosenstein-Rodan' (1972).

[3] Bhaduri, Amit, op. cit.

Bardhan has considered a model of dualistic agriculture by taking into account the imperfections of the labour and the credit market. Imperfection of the labour market, in his analysis, arises due to the gap that exists between the wage rate in the capitalist farm and the marginal product of labour in the family farm, and this imperfection can be regarded as working in favour of the family farm. Imperfection of the credit market, on the other hand, is reflected in the fact that it is possible to get cheaper credit with the increase in the wealth position of the borrower, and wealth here is identified with a composite factor of production, called land-capital. The source of this credit has been left exogenous in this model, but it is clear that the capitalist farm has a comparative advantage in the credit market because, unlike the family farm, it can save and this saving is always turned into the accumulation of land-capital (a consequence of the assumption that land-capital is the only asset), thus increasing the base for cheaper credit. This credit is then used by the capitalist farm to buy a category of inputs which is the vehicle of land-augmenting technical progress, so that the imperfection of credit market is finally reflected in the capitalist farm having a cheaper access to technical progress. This advantage of imperfect credit market, because of the continuous accumulation of land-capital, is essentially a dynamic one and it is shown how, under certain assumptions on the production function and the nature of technical progress, this dynamic advantage can dominate the purely static advantage of the labour market imperfection over time and thus make the income of the capitalist farm grow relatively faster than the income of the family farm.

This model of Bardhan is remarkably elegant in its formal structure, but it leaves certain questions unanswered. Apart from certain minor points, such as the apparent sensitivity of the conclusions to the particular form (namely, Cobb-Douglas) of the production function considered, the more serious question relates to the assumption of the existence of only asset in the form of land-capital. Since the implication of this assumption is that whatever is saved is automatically turned into accumulation of capital, one cannot, under such assumption, pose any problem of insufficient capital accumulation. What Bardhan has done, therefore, really amounts to sidetracking the question of stagnation in capital accumulation in a dualistic agriculture and considering instead the question of the distribution of income in the context of a hypothetical growth process of such agriculture. However, in view of the persisting problem of insufficiency of capital accumulation in many dualistic agriculture, of evidence to the effect that saving by certain groups of farmers has not automatically been transformed into capital accumulation, we have found it more important to address ourselves to this existing problem of stagnation and see to what extent it is related to the question of income distribution.

In posing this problem we have developed a comprehensive model of dualistic agriculture by taking into account all its major characteristics relating to, among others, the state of its distribution of income and the structure of market, and including, in particular, the possibility of existence of two forms of holding of wealth in terms of capital and loan. We have seen that in terms of this model it is possible to provide an explanation of the problem of inadequate capital accumulation of this kind of agriculture, an explanation which also brings out the crucial importance of income distribution in this matter.

Turning to Bhaduri's paper, one should note, first of all, that it does not strictly relate to the problem of a dualistic agriculture in the sense we have defined it. It relates to what he calls "a semi-feudal" agriculture which is characterised in his analysis by the existence of two income groups—the sharecroppers and the landowners. The sharecropper works on the land owned by the landowner for a fixed share of the harvest, and he also takes consumption loan from the same landowner. The problem of portfolio choice that is inherent in such a situation has not been clearly stated in the model, but through the specification of technical progress, Bhaduri has made the landowner face a problem of conflict between the two sources of income, interest earnings and the income from harvest, which is similar in spirit to the problem encountered by the capitalist farm in the presence of technical progress in our model. This concept of conflict is then used by Bhaduri to interpret in a very interesting and insightful way the historical forces that may be taking shape in certain parts of India.

The difficulty which we have found with Bhaduri's paper, however, is that there are certain crucial issues which are never explained in economic terms. It is not clear, for example, why the sharecropper will never go for production loan even if his income is above the subsistence level and the productivity of land-capital is increasing due to technical progress. It should be noted that the final conclusion of the paper about the inevitability of a conflict between the two sources of income of the landowner is not quite independent of the way this issue is resolved. To say that such issues are settled politically is perhaps to leave them economically underexplained. The more interesting line of enquiry may be to try to find out whether there are any basic economic forces at work which make such supposedly political solutions what they are. In fact, in the case of this corner solution involving the consumption loan, we have seen that it is indeed possible to give an explanation on the basis of rational economic decision making on the part of the family and capitalist farms.

References

Bardhan Pranab, K. (1972). A Model of Growth of Capitalism in a Dual Agrarian Economy. In J. Bagwati & R. Eckhaus (Eds.), *Essays in Honour of Rosenstein-Rodan*. Abingdon: Routledge.

Sen, A. K. (October 1966). Peasants and Dualism with or Without Surplus Labour. *Journal of Political Economy, 74,* 425–450.

CHAPTER 8

Generalisations

Abstract Several ways of generalising the basic model have been considered in this final chapter, by relaxing (a) the simplifying assumptions that have been made about the agricultural sector itself and (b) the ones made about the relationship between the agricultural and the industrial sector. It is shown that even after these generalisations, most of the important conclusions of the basic model remain unimpaired.

Keywords Relaxation of assumptions • Agriculture-industry relation • Landless labourers • Structure of the industrial sector

It is possible to generalise our basic analytical model in two directions: by relaxing (a) the simplifying assumptions that were made about the agricultural sector itself and (b) the ones made about the relationship between the agricultural and industrial sectors. We shall mention some of these possibilities very briefly.

1. The landless labourers were not included in the description of the initial state of the model. This, however, is not any restrictive assumption, because it has been shown that the model, starting with an initial state involving the family and capitalist farms, will itself evolve in a way that the landowners of family farms, through a process of immiserisation, will be found converted into the landless labourers. In other words, the landless labourer can always be accommodated

into our discussion as representing a particular stage in the evolution of the model. However, if we also want to explain why some of the landowners of the family farms may become landless labourers faster than others, so that at some point of time in history, there can exist the family farm, the capitalist farm, and also the landless labourer, we will have to allow for some variation among the family farms themselves, say, in terms of their landownership, in the description of the initial state.

2. To simplify calculations, the parameter μ was assumed to be constant. This assumption, however, can be relaxed and the implications of a variation in μ analysed. We have seen in Chapter 3 that m can be considered as depending on L_2 and $\bar{L}_2 : \mu = \mu(L_2, \bar{L}_2)$ with $\partial \mu / \partial L_2 > 0$ (opportunity cost) and $\partial \mu / \partial \bar{L}_2 < 0$ (economies of scale). Since $d\bar{L}_2/dt > 0$ and it is expected that $dL_2/dt > 0$, the sign of m can go in either direction. If $d\mu/dt < 0$, then there will be yet another force to depress the value of y_1 and as a result the tendency towards stagnation will only be strengthened. On the other hand, if $d\mu/dt > 0$ and if w also increases corresponding to that, the effect will be similar to the one that followed from the family farms collectively bargaining for wages. However, given the characterisation of the initial state in terms of a slow rate of capital accumulation, it is unlikely that the effect of an increase in L_2 will be strong enough to overcome the corresponding effect of an increase in $\bar{L}_2$, so that the initial behaviour of μ is more likely to be as in the first situation. And, then, with its negative feedback on capital accumulation, it is also possible that the downward tendency of µ and of capital accumulation may start reinforcing each other without the second possibility, $d\mu/dt > 0$, ever getting materialised.

3. Technical progress was assumed in our model to be exogenous and the reason was again essentially to simplify algebra. It is possible to endogenise technological progress by adding another input, to represent, say, the category of biochemical inputs, into the production function and then regarding that input as the vehicle of technical progress. The allocational decision with respect to this input will be essentially similar to that of capital; only the number of equations and variables will increase.

4. It may be recalled that in the description of the initial state of the model, the labour market, unlike the credit market, was not assumed to be segmented. However, as a consequence of imperfection in the credit market and the possibility of non-repayment of loan, it is

possible for this initial state in the labour market to be replaced by localised monopsony requiring that the family farms supply their labour to the local capitalist farm. In the face of non-repayment of loan, imperfection of credit market may also give rise to monopsony in the commodity market in the sense that the family farms may have to sell their output to the capitalist farm at a price lower than the competitive market price. This kind of monopsonisation, for one thing, may represent additional institutional means through which the process of immiserisation of the family farm will go on. For another, by reducing the number of sellers in the commodity market, it may also give rise to some form of regionally localised monopolistic competition in the commodity market, in which case a part of the burden may also be shifted to the consumers outside the agricultural sector.

5. It is possible to include some other institutional forms of agriculture within the basic structure of our analysis. Inclusion of sharecropping, for example, will alter some of the allocation rules, but it can be shown, and here some of the results of Bhaduri's model can be profitably used, that the basic tendencies of the agricultural sector will not change in their qualitative properties. In the same vein, a more interesting generalisation can be made if the money lenders and the capitalist farmers are considered as two separate classes. In a sense, it is somewhat difficult to visualise this situation, because it is not clear why, given an unequal distribution of income and the assured profitability of an imperfect credit market, a capitalist farmer will not consider money lending as another source of income. But if, because of reasons of uncertainty or some other non-economic consideration, for example, the influence of the caste system, such a separation really exists, then it will have a significant effect in eliminating some of the sources of conflict responsible for the agricultural stagnation.

6. Finally, the results obtained exclusively within the agricultural sector can be generalised to accommodate the interactions with the industrial sector. The basic characteristics of this industrial sector have been outlined in Chapter 2. It is known to be partitioned into a private sector producing consumer goods and a government sector producing capital goods. The product as well as the credit market of this sector will have characteristics of imperfection. The imperfection of the product market will be implied in the properties of the

relevant average revenue curve, whereas the credit market imperfection will be reflected by the dependence of the terms of borrowing on the wealth of the borrower. Because of the existence of these two kinds of imperfection at the same time, it will be found that a problem of conflict will again arise in the decision making about industrial expansion, and this conflict will have some similarity with the one faced by the capitalist farm in agriculture.

Given this structure of the industrial sector, its two most important links with agriculture will be through the commodity market and the labour market. The labour market link can be characterised by a Harris-Todaro type of migration mechanism, and product market by an expression of terms of trade involving the price and the income elasticities of the sectoral demand and supply functions. The interaction through labour market will have the effect of making the rate of growth of labour supply, g, dependent on the effects of the industrial sector, whereas the impact of product market interaction will be felt in terms of the variation of $\bar{P}$. With these variations in g and appropriately characterised, it will be possible to generalise the allocation rules of our basic model, which were initially derived with constant g and, to accommodate these variations and, through them, the interacting effects of the industrial sector.

Index[1]

A

Agriculture
 credit market, 2, 4, 5, 8–10, 50, 56, 57
 dualistic, 9, 10, 25, 27, 29, 34, 46, 47, 50–52, 56–60, 67, 69–71
 interaction with industry, 4, 75, 76
 labour and National Sample Survey (2013), 4n2
 labour market monopsony, 4, 9, 25, 61, 70, 74–76
 landless agricultural labourers, 4n2, 60, 61
 production process, 5

B

Bardhan, Pranab K., 18n7, 61, 69, 69n2, 70
Bhaduri, Amit, 67n5, 69, 69n3, 71, 75
Bhagwati, J., 17n6, 66n4, 69n2
Bowles, S., 66n4

C

Capitalist farm's allocational decisions, 1, 6, 9, 11, 24, 26, 58
Chakravarty, S., 17n6

D

Distribution of income and capital accumulation, 47, 49, 51–58, 70, 71
Dualistic agriculture overtime, 9, 10, 27, 29, 34, 46, 47, 50–52, 56–60, 67, 69–71

F

Family farm's allocational decision, 2, 6, 10, 11, 25, 58

I

Industrial sector, characteristics of, 1, 3, 4, 69, 73, 75, 76

---

[1] Note: Page numbers followed by 'n' refer to notes.

© The Author(s) 2018
A. K. Dasgupta, *Income Distribution, Market Imperfections and Capital Accumulation in a Developing Economy*,
https://doi.org/10.1007/978-981-13-1633-3

L
Land reforms and capital accumulation, 53, 61

M
Migration and wage gap, 4, 17–19, 19n8

S
Sen, Amartya K., x, 17n6, 69, 69n1
Socio-cultural factors, effects of, 58

Stagnation of dualistic agriculture, 10, 51, 58–60, 67, 70
Stiglitz, Joseph E., 19n8

T
Technical progress and its effects, 64–68, 70

V
Various generalisations, 73–76

Printed in the USA
CPSIA information can be obtained
at www.ICGtesting.com
CBHW060335230924
14770CB00005B/264